189

ways to contact God

189

ways to contact God

MARLENE HALPIN, O.P.

CHICAGO

3441 North Ashland Avenue
Chicago, Illinois 60657

Interior design by Mary Bowers

Library of Congress Cataloging-in-Publication Data

Halpin, Marlene.
189 ways to contact God/Marlene Halpin.
p. cm.
ISBN 0-8294-1365-0 (pbk.)
1. Prayer—Christianity. I. Title. II. Title: One hundred eighty nine ways to contact God.
BV210.2.H3516 1999 99-26830
242'.8—DC21 CIP

Printed in the United States of America

99 00 01 02 03 / 10 9 8 7 6 5 4 3 2 1

This book is dedicated to all those who yearn for God, whether they are aware of it or not, and to all those whose love for God is real in their lives and in their prayer, whether they recognize it or not.

CONTENTS

ACKNOWLEDGMENTS

A word of thanks

~ to Loyola Press, who extended the invitation to write of ways to pray "for people in the pew";

~ to those gracious editors: LaVonne Neff, Vinita Hampton Wright, and Barbara Campbell, whose courteous enthusiasm made this project a joy;

~ to the many people who generously spoke about the ways they pray: the Holtgreive family, the Masseys, and the Kerneys; Fathers James Kerndt, O.C.S.O., and Ken Schmidt; Rev. Dr. Waldemar Schmeichel; Dr. Michael Graf and Dr. Dick Bower; Sisters Helen Battle, S.S.J., Joy Castiglione, O.P., Nancy Goult, O.P., Ann Lockwood, O.P., Sue McCrery, S.S.J., Sherry Pesch, O.C.S.O., Andrea Sieloff, R.S.M., Irene Weiner, O.P., and Cecilia Werner, O.P.; Bob Badra, Barbara Bauman, Janet Baumgartner, Jane Bodway, Ann Fitzpatrick Boltz, Rosemary Cleveland, John Giannini, Mona Heppe, Tom Rea, and the participants of the Ministry Formation Program of the Diocese of Kalamazoo.

May Yahweh find joy in what he creates.
Psalm 104:31 (JB)

HOW TO USE THIS BOOK

First, let me explain what this book is not. It's not a book on why we should pray. We already know that we need to pray. Neither is it a book about where to pray, although some good suggestions come up.

This is not a collection of prayers. There are books and books of those already.

This book is about how to pray. The expectation is that you will recognize yourself on some of the pages or that you will find some ways to get started. I also expect that you will grow far beyond these methods to wherever the Holy Spirit leads you. And I hope that you will find great satisfaction in your growing relationship with God.

Second, let me say some words about communication. Often the quality of a relationship relies on the quality of communication between two people. How communication happens is as varied, as personal, as idiosyncratic as each of us is and as we are together.

So it is between our God and us. Prayer is about communication.

Communication experts tend to list levels of communication in the following ways:

- the "good morning, how are you, have a nice day" kind of thing you might say in passing;
- the "hope my team wins, wish we'd see some sun for a change, can't wait for deer-hunting season" sort of weather and sports talk;
- the gossipy "did you see what she's wearing? know what I heard he did last night? where do you think they went on vacation?" prattle about other people;
- the "I feel (hurt, baffled, frightened, delirious with joy, vindicated, hateful, glad, sorry)" declaration from the heart about situations or happenings in your life;
- the kind of communication that happens from knowing and loving the other person and the other person knowing and loving you. There is a genuine and deep comfort, trust, union—perhaps even synergy and communion—between you. Here is the joy of a truly good friend.

Probably each of us can name people in our lives who fit on this or that level. Now for the hard part. Forget about what you desire or intend to do. In cold reality, consider:

- In my everyday living, honestly and truthfully, on what level is my communication with God?
- In my everyday living, honestly and truthfully, what is the depth of my relationship with God?

These questions can be answered best, and with greatest honesty, in the loving presence of God, in the depths of your soul. Although the self-assessment might leave you dissatisfied, the joy of it is this:

~ God is with us.
~ God invites us to closer union.
~ God's grace makes it possible.

All that is needed is for us, individually, to say yes to God. Jesus reveals how to do this. Jesus promises that if we ask, we shall receive the living water, the Holy Spirit. Let us recognize our need, ask, and consent to God's action in our lives, in God's way.

It is not always easy. But it is simple. It is most fulfilling and deeply peaceful, because it is what God wants for us.

These prayer suggestions provide various ways to start—or to continue—to abide in God.

May God, who begins this good work in us, bring it to a happy conclusion.

PRAYER FROM THE FAMILIAR

People need to worship God, not only in private, but also as a people, publicly. For that we are offered ritual and ceremony, means of satisfying the human spirit. The greatest public worship in the Catholic Church is the celebration of the Liturgy of the Eucharist.

Some of the prayers are fixed and always prayed with formality and with eloquence. Other prayers change according to the season and the feast being celebrated. During the cycle of a year, we are reminded of the birth, life, teachings, death, and resurrection of Jesus; of the necessity of forgiving and asking for forgiveness; of the call to receive God's loving mercy; and of the incessant plea for unity among us.

Sometimes (often, I hope) a word, a phrase, or a prayer strikes your heart with its meaning or precipitates an insight that affects you. That experience is best followed up in private prayer or conversation. Pursue it; pray from it.

The pages in this section are examples of what struck some worshipers during their participation in the Liturgy of the Eucharist.

May you be ever more conscious of how these prayers might affect you. Let them make your life more abundant.

I

THE SIGN OF THE CROSS

In some Christian denominations, religious ceremonies and times of prayer are begun and ended with a gesture and prayer called the Sign of the Cross. Most commonly it is made by placing the left hand on the heart, gesturing with the right hand from forehead to breast, to left shoulder, to right shoulder, then bringing the hands together.

While making the Sign of the Cross, remember that it brings to mind our triune God. You may want to meditate while making it:

"In the name of the Father," your creating God who brings all into being and keeps all in being, whose splendid love makes all good. As you touch your forehead, dedicate to God your knowledge, your thoughts, your plans, and your obligations.

"and of the Son," your redeeming God who gives us Jesus. As you touch your breast, bring to God your loves, your affections, and your desires.

"and of the Holy Spirit," your sanctifying God whose love makes you holy if you allow it. As you touch your shoulders, bring to God your going and your coming back, with all the people and events of those movements and your concerns about them.

"Amen." So be it, to the best of your ability, safe in God's care.

2

"PEACE BE WITH YOU"

Peace be with you."

"And also with you." These words are exchanged at every liturgy. Sometimes they are followed by a gesture as people wish each other peace.

What about *your* peace—the peace, or lack of it, within yourself?

The classical definition of peace is "the tranquillity of order." When this prayer is said for you—first by the celebrant, then by your neighbors—might you look at your heart and ask, *Where, among my relationships, is there not peace? Where is there not tranquillity because something offensive, something not forgiven, blocks it?*

When that prayer is said for you, examine your heart. Bring to God's presence someone with whom you are not at peace. Pray for that person. Forgive that person, if you can. Ask for help to forgive that person if you cannot yet do it. And let peace be ever more deeply yours.

3

"I CONFESS"

Right at the beginning of the liturgy, the most sacred of the community's prayers, you prepare yourself. Before entering into the sacredness of the ceremony and celebrating the mysteries of your salvation, you take steps to come as worthily as you can—but not alone.

After the greeting, you look at what in your life needs attention. And so you begin:

"I confess to almighty God,
and to you, my brothers and sisters,
that I have sinned."

Do you ever notice that you do not, in this particular prayer, call God "you"? You say, "to almighty God" and "to you, my brothers and sisters" and go on about sin, in thought and in word, in what was done and in what was not done. The community can pray this, honestly, together. The particulars of your sins you might attend to with God privately.

At the end, you ask for help. From whom? "Blessed Mary, . . . / the angels and saints, / and you, my brothers and sisters."

Stop a moment and think. What a magnificent family! What an array of people on whom you can call for help! God's mother, the angels and saints (all those who are in God's eternal presence), and all of the rest of us (our brothers and sisters) who are still struggling.

What a support group! And the other side of it is that everyone at church is asking for *your* help.

So you pray in and with the strength of all the other praying people present.

What do you want to say to God about that?

4

"LORD, HAVE MERCY"

At the beginning of the liturgy you pray, "Lord, have mercy," then "Christ, have mercy." Do you believe mercy will be given to you?

People tend to think, at times, that God wouldn't forgive this or couldn't forgive that. That they aren't worth God's bother. So they pray these words "have mercy" routinely, not really believing them.

In your prayer you might want to let these words, with their meaning, seep into your consciousness, into your very being.

"Lord, have mercy."

"But," you might protest, "isn't the Lord also just?"

Yes. But consider this: Mercy flows from love. God is love. Love is God's very being. Take a few moments to let that understanding fill you. Then take a few more to remind yourself that God loves you—unconditionally.

God is just. Why is justice required? Because of the wrongdoing of God's creatures, us. Now let yourself ponder this: Justice is needed because of a creature's sin. Mercy comes from God's being (love).

What's greater, God, or a creature's wrongdoing? What's more important?

The next time you pray, "Lord, have mercy. Christ, have mercy," let your heart and soul be full of the gratitude and joy that are God's gifts to you.

5

"THE LORD, THE GIVER OF LIFE"

When you pray the Nicene Creed, either in private or during public worship, you might want to reflect on the different parts of it. The creeds are the result of a great deal of study, prayer, and reflection, all aimed at saying briefly and clearly what Christians truly believe.

At the moment the question is, do *you* believe this? If you do, what difference does it make to you? How does it affect the way you live? What makes you want to get up in the morning; what gives satisfaction and gladness to your day?

For instance (any phrase will do; pick your own), try this one on for size:

"We believe in the Holy Spirit, the Lord, the giver of life."

The Holy Spirit is the Spirit of love, the Spirit of Jesus, the One Jesus sends to complete his own mission:

I have come to bring *life* and life in *abundance* (see John 10:10).

Is your life one of abundance? If so, give thanks! If not, and if you do "believe in the Holy Spirit, the Lord, the giver of life," ask for help.

Sometimes not asking for help is what impoverishes your life. Sometimes not asking for help for the down-deep things is what makes life look bleak and hardly worth living.

"The Lord, the giver of life," is there, ever ready and most eager to help.

Ask! Be willing to receive what God wants to give you.

6

"THE LORD BE WITH YOU"

"The Lord be with you."

"And also with you."

Know with your whole being that the Lord *is* with you. Take a few moments to let yourself be quite conscious of the marvelous reality that the Lord is with you.

Before going to work, pray: *Lord, be with me*. Believe it is so.

Before attending a meeting, pray: *Lord, be with me*. Believe it is so.

Before starting another day of caregiving, pray: *Lord, be with me*. Believe it is so.

For, always and everywhere, the Lord *is* with you.

7

"LIFT UP YOUR HEARTS"

During the liturgy the priest prays out loud:

"Lift up your hearts."

The people respond:

"We lift them up to the Lord."

Do you?

Do you lift up
- ~ your heart, full of praise and thanks to your God for making you, and making you good;
- ~ your heart, glad, troubled, angry, exhausted, ho-hum;
- ~ your heart, brimming with love or longing;
- ~ your heart, however it is?

When you hear these words, "Lift up your hearts," do it! Give God your heart for healing, for filling even fuller with love for God and for the people in your life.

8

"HOLY, HOLY, HOLY"

You pray, "Holy, holy, holy Lord."

What do you mean when you say those words?

Maybe the grandeur of God is striking you. Praise God if this is so. God's grandeur elicits awe. God is awe-full. Say it from your heart: holy, holy, holy!

Just what does *holy* mean?

Holy is whole, entire, complete, simple, sacred, single-hearted, good. God is God. There is nothing bad about God, nothing tempting God or pulling God into parts, or un-wholeness. That utter and absolute simplicity of who is God is dazzling in its purity.

You may read or talk about being "integrated." Being one inside yourself, at peace. Something in you calls you to be simple, single-hearted, good. You may strive for this peace in your life. Even with God's help, it is often a struggle to make choices, consistently, that help you become at one with God and with yourself.

Perhaps a plea for your own holiness is implicit in this prayer. But when you pray it, pray with your whole being in awe, in praise, in adoration, naming your God as . . .

Holy, holy, holy!

9

"WE THANK YOU FOR COUNTING US WORTHY"

To accomplish great things, great people are wanted.

To be in the company of great people is an honor, an honor of which many people think themselves unworthy. Just think of how excited people are when they meet a famous person, when they see a well-known person, when they happen to be in an elevator with a celebrity. Don't they talk about it a great deal? It is something they do not take for granted. For some, it is their moment of glory.

Let yourself think about GOD. (It might help to think of what *only* God can be, of what *only* God can do. If you are even nearly right, you will be in awe.)

As you remain in awe of God, listen to the words of the second eucharistic prayer:

"We thank you for counting us worthy
to stand in your presence and serve you."

"We thank you" The pronoun *we* excludes no one. No wonder the liturgy begins with all acknowledging together their sin. No wonder everyone needs the sign of peace during liturgy!

"for counting us worthy" Start with yourself. Worthy? Spend time with your God and consider the magnitude of the invitation.

"to stand in your presence" Let the reality of that go through you. Pray from it as your heart desires.

"and serve you." How? How might this affect your attitude toward helping others—all those included in "we thank you"?

You might do well to take this prayer home with you and continue it later.

10

"A LIVING SACRIFICE OF PRAISE"

Listen with your mind and heart to the fourth eucharistic prayer. Part of it reads:

"By your Holy Spirit, gather all who share this bread and wine
into the one body of Christ, a living sacrifice of praise."

Of course, such a great work ("into the one body of Christ, a living sacrifice") has to be the work of the Holy Spirit. Only God can accomplish that! But take a moment, if you will, to think about "a living sacrifice of praise." What might that mean for you?

Sacrifice has two basic meanings. First, it means that you give yourself. Realistically, how do you give yourself to God? What does that mean for you? (There's a good thing to talk about with God!) Second, sacrifice means dying. It means dying to the false self, to those things that are not truly you. It can be words or behaviors, decisions or relationships that are real but are not right. A certain part of you may enjoy that false self (think of addictions, bad habits, certain pleasures or relationships). A deeper, truer part of you would be embarrassed if those actions became known publicly. You would be ashamed because, while they are pleasing, they are wrong. And you know it. This prayer calls for a sacrifice of them, a dying to them, in praise of God, who made you, and made you good. Dying is followed by rising—to new life.

This prayer takes some attention, doesn't it?

II

"DELIVER US, LORD"

In each of the four Gospels, Jesus says not to be afraid. He talks about not being anxious, not being troubled. He speaks of God's constant care for you.

Attend to the powerful prayer right after the Lord's Prayer:

"Deliver us, Lord, from every evil,
and grant us peace in our day.
In your mercy keep us free from sin
and protect us from all anxiety."

Attend to these strong words. Let them sink into you. Ask God, truly, for protection from the evil things you know in your own life and in the lives of those you love ("Deliver us, Lord, from every evil") as well as the evils of which you might not yet be aware.

Attend to these powerful words, asking to be healed and liberated from those things that lead you and those you love into sin ("In your mercy keep us free from sin").

And then, delivered from outside evils and kept from inside sins, how well it follows that you be protected "from all anxiety." Do you allow God to do this for you?

If you pray this prayer with all your heart, you will more fully pray its glorious conclusion:

"For the kingdom, the power, and the glory are yours, now and for ever."

Take this prayer seriously. Be glad in God's mercy, God's protection, God's freeing you from anxiety.

12

"LOOK NOT"

Look not on our sins, but on the faith of your Church."

Why do you think God should grant this favor? Perhaps there is a clue in the remainder of the request:

"and grant us the peace and unity of your kingdom where you live for ever and ever."

What strength there is in this!

Notice that the prayer does not say "my" sins or "my" faith; nor does it grant "me" peace. Everything is plural. Everything is the prayer of the community for the community. You are not alone. You are not alone in sin nor in faith. Nor are you alone in peace and in unity. Always there is the community. Strength beyond your personal strength goes into the prayer. Please don't forget that *your* personal strength and prayer are also needed by the community.

"Look not on our sins, but on the faith of your Church."

Remember that the Church is the people of God, of whom you are one. You are asking this favor for everyone, and everyone is asking for you. That must be powerful before God!

In God's presence, ponder more deeply the real meaning of this prayer. Look at the implications of "Look not on our sins." Remember, you are asking God to look at *your* faith as well as your neighbor's.

Pray out of this prayer as your heart desires. (You do not need words. Show your mind and heart to your God.) Be quiet before God with an open heart.

13

"LET US OFFER EACH OTHER THE SIGN OF PEACE"

With these words, the celebrant invites you to acknowledge one another. This invitation extends the prayer that just asked God, "Look not on our sins, but on the faith of your Church, / and grant us the peace and unity of your kingdom." Now the people of God are called upon to offer each other a sign of peace and unity.

Every person needs to receive from and contribute to the community. (Remember the words "I will take you as my people, and I will be your God" [Exodus 6:7]?) Jesus came for *all* people. (Even the angels announced that to the shepherds!) Jesus died to save *all* people. In this vein you greet one another.

You need to worship God as one of a people, a community. The Liturgy of the Eucharist provides a most sacred means to do that. Within it, you are asked to offer a sign of peace to your neighbor.

~ When might you not want the invitation?
~ What might this invitation require of you?

~ What is the overriding factor in whether and how you greet another at this time?

Be honest with God. Be honest about how sincerely you join Jesus' prayer for peace and unity. Ask your God for what you need to be a good part of the people of God.

14

"LAMB OF GOD"

Before receiving the Eucharist during the liturgy, the priest prays: "Lamb of God, you take away the sins of the world: have mercy on us . . . grant us peace."

As you look at the host with the eyes of faith, let the meaning of it seep through you.

"Have mercy." Realize that God knows you, understands what you have done and left undone, and in mercy loves and welcomes you (think of the father in the parable of the prodigal son). Respond to your God's understanding and love.

"Grant us peace." Peace: the tranquillity of order. Ask God to put right order in your decisions, in your relationships, in all of your life. (It might mean letting grudges go.)

Again, with the eyes of faith, look at the host. Try to realize the magnitude of God's gift in the Eucharist.

Let your prayer after communion include what God does for you, what God offers you in this great gift, and what your response will be.

15

"THIS IS MY BODY. . . . THIS IS MY BLOOD"

When the priest prays this prayer over the bread and the wine, Catholic doctrine teaches that the elements are changed into the very body and blood of Jesus, the Christ.

Probably you were taught that a long time ago. Perhaps it was one of those things you took on faith.

Maybe now, with your age and experience, you wonder about it.

If so, the immortal prayer of the father of a child to Jesus could be made yours:

"I believe; help my unbelief!" (Mark 9:24).

Pray that, since this gift is infinitely beyond the methods of our scientific age, you will go beyond understanding it. Move from wondering *about* it to wondering *at* it. Thanks and praise will come from you easily then. Stay with it. God does good and great things.

16

"LORD, I AM NOT WORTHY"

Just before receiving communion you pray:

"Lord, I am not worthy to receive you,
but only say the word and I shall be healed."

People, of themselves, are not worthy to receive (not take, but *receive*) the Lord into their very being. Yet that is the offer made to you.

Asking, out of your unworthiness, to be healed is in itself a worthy prayer. Every time you receive communion, you ask for healing. What malady of your spirit do you present to the Lord?

Might you think, every time, of naming the disorder you want healed so that you are in fact more worthy to receive your Lord in so intimate a way?

When Jesus asked people what they wanted of him, and they told him, his next question was, "Do *you* believe?"

When you ask, "But only say the word and I shall be healed," do you believe?

Go before your God as you are, and ask for what you need. In the asking, let yourself be aware that it is the Holy One you are petitioning—and why.

17

RECEIVING COMMUNION

When you receive Holy Communion, what do you do?

You approach the sanctuary. The Sacred Host is held in front of you while you are reminded: "The body of Christ." And you reply, "Amen."

You hold out your hand, palm upward, cradled in your other hand. In a symbolic way you make a throne of your hands to receive your Lord. The Sacred Host is placed in your hand. The Lord comes.

You swallow the Sacred Host and spend some time in prayer with the Lord, the bread of life who has come to bring you life.

How simple! How ordinary the actions! How extraordinary the meaning!

How easy Jesus makes it for people to receive him. The Gospels tell you that Jesus' enemies chided him for eating with publicans and sinners. With everyone. With you.

You might want to recall Jesus' saying, "Everything that the Father gives me will come to me, and anyone who comes to me I will never drive away" (John 6:37).

Ponder these words of Jesus. Hear them spoken to you. How does your heart want to pray?

Let your spirit rest in the One who loves you so dearly and faithfully.

18

"GO IN PEACE TO LOVE AND SERVE THE LORD"

At the end of the liturgy the celebrant says to the people: "Go in peace to love and serve the Lord."

In response the people pray:

"Thanks be to God."

During the liturgy you have prayed for forgiveness, for unity, for your and others' needs. So strengthened, you are sent forth to serve others.

Serve others? This may be in large, important ways. You may have a job that is one of service. Then, perhaps, you might concentrate on how to make your service more effective and pleasant. More often your service is in the small, courteous, thoughtful ways that occur with each person you encounter during the day. (Don't forget your family members and colleagues!)

Of course you are not going to succeed perfectly. All sorts of human things distract and deter you and those you would serve. But the prayer says, "Go in peace."

Know that whatever your successes, whatever your failures, you can return. In the returning, your healing continues.

For your merciful and loving God is always present, welcoming and encouraging you.

"Go in peace to love and serve the Lord."

How does your heart want to pray?

19

A PRAYER FOR ALL SITUATIONS

Many of the official prayers of the Church are formal, eloquent, elegant, majestic. So they should be.

Many people, especially when life is difficult, pray more immediately from their here-and-now, earthly experience. Liturgy provides that too.

If you are praying as a person
~ who works with machinery
~ who works on a farm
~ who works in an office cubicle
~ who is a health-care professional
~ who is an executive
~ who is a street person
~ who is a gang member
~ who has children with incessant demands
~ who is a caregiver
how do you articulate your experience of God?

If you are praying from
~ a hospital
~ a home
~ a prison
~ an inner-city ghetto
~ a subway
~ a lonely place
how do you articulate your experience of God?

If you are praying as a person
~ who is surrounded by loving family and friends
~ who is rejected by anyone who might mean something to you
~ who is just plain lonely and unsuccessful
how do you articulate your experience of God?

One prayer cuts through all of the variables. One prayer, in stark simplicity, says what you need to say:

"Lord, have mercy.
Christ, have mercy.
Lord, have mercy."

Be confident. The Lord has mercy for you, for all.

PRAYER IN THE DAILY THINGS

20

BATHING

Some of us are caregivers—for a child or for an older person, such as a parent, spouse, or friend. Perhaps one of our responsibilities is bathing the person. This task can become a lovely time of intimacy, a time when touch can be infused with prayer.

It may be silent prayer. We can pray for the person whose body is being cleaned and comforted. We can intercede for that person's needs. We can ask for that person what God wants to give, and we can pray that the person will receive God's gift. We can ask for ourselves whatever we need to continue giving care in these circumstances.

This might be a good time to tell God that you trust this "work unto good." It might surprise you what good things come of it.

21

BLESSING

A blessing affirms one in being.

Every night when your child goes to bed, bless him or her (perhaps making the Sign of the Cross on the child's forehead), saying:

"May God bless you.
I love you."

If something special is going on, perhaps add:

"May God bless you and comfort you.
May God bless you and strengthen you.
May God bless you and be glad in you."

The day might come when the child blesses you back!

22

COOKING

Cooking is so obviously a time for prayer!

For whom do you cook? Your family? Your housemate? Your community? Yourself?

If you cook for others, be conscious of God's presence and think of each of them as you shop for groceries and prepare food. Let God know that you are grateful for them (or if not, why not). Put each of them in your heart and, together with your God, love them. Just love them!

Ask God to bless each of them.

Ask God to give each of them what God wants to give.

Ask God to help them receive God's gift.

Then rest in God's love for them—and you.

23

FISHING

Assuming that you fish for sport, not as a basic means of livelihood, why do you do it?

If you like to go fishing (or ice fishing) alone, why do you do it? Take a moment to think of half a dozen reasons. You need to get away. You need to be alone. Tell yourself what you get out of it.

If you like to go fishing with another person, take a moment to explain to yourself why you enjoy the companionship. Give yourself several reasons. If you are honest, some of the reasons might surprise you. Some of them you might not want to say out loud. That's normal.

Now let God know why—*really* why—you like to go fishing, alone or with a companion. Explore it with God. (You don't need words, you know. God can know your thoughts with you. Your feelings, also.)

Then be with God in a way that is helpful or enjoyable or in some way right for you.

24

IRONING

When ironing, look at the garment you are pressing.

As you smooth out the wrinkles, go to God in your heart and ask:

What wrinkles in me do you want to smooth out?

And listen. Honestly listen.

Or look at the garment you are ironing.

Look, in your mind and heart, at the person who wears it.

Together with your God, look at the person who wears it.

And together, love that person.

25

TELEPHONE

The phone rings.

Before answering (friend? telemarketer? colleague?) or before looking at Caller ID, say a quick prayer.

Ask God to bless you and the person on the other end of the line.

Ask God to make you peaceful and pleasant.

Ask God to help you respond well to the other person. How well? Well enough so that if you saw God there with you, you would know that your response is right for the other person and for you.

The good part is that you don't need words. (If you stopped that long, the phone probably would stop ringing!) God knows your mind and heart. Dart the prayer to God. You both know what it means.

26

ROCKING

"I don't have time to pray!"

If you are the parent of a baby, you know that this little presence dramatically affects your lifestyle. Caring for a little one's constant needs can really eat into the twenty-four hours of your day. What can you do about taking care of your baby and praying?

Suppose you are breast-feeding. Isn't it possible for you to hold your baby, rock your baby, cuddle your baby, love your baby, and feed your baby—and be in prayer at the same time? Use the care-for-baby time to ask God to bless your child. What can you ask for your baby? What can you ask for yourself or for others you love?

Suppose you are rocking your child to sleep. Can you not hold and cuddle your baby and, while rocking your baby to sleep, simultaneously be in God's presence? Asking for what you, your baby, and your family need? Offering to God whatever you want to offer as thanks for this child?

While nursing, rocking, and in other circumstances, you can immerse yourself in God's love. You can know, in these and other times, that God is, at this very moment, loving you and your child. Allow yourself to *know* God's presence, God's delight in you and in your child. And, with God, love this baby in this moment.

What a gift for your child!

What a gift for you!

27

TRAFFIC LIGHTS

Whether you're driving or walking, you often have to pause at traffic lights. A traffic-light pause is a good time for a brief prayer.

If you have prayed from Scripture and were struck by a line or two, use that as a "reminding" prayer during the day. *O Lord, I know you are near. . . . Lord Jesus, I do believe. Help thou my unbelief. . . . Do you love me?* Use whatever stays in your mind and heart from Sunday or from your private prayer. Remember it and whisper it while waiting for the light to change.

Or if you have a mantra (a short prayer you say often: *My God and my all . . . Jesus, have mercy on me. . . . I am with you always. . . . Come, Holy Spirit, come),* pray it while waiting for the light to change.

28

CLEANING

One of the good things about cleaning (especially bathrooms and kitchens) is that you see a difference. There's a certain satisfaction in being able to say, "That's done!"

When your home is clean and straightened up, you might be tired, but you're probably pleased. You know it won't stay clean for long. You can count on all the dust to come back. But for the moment, things are fine.

While you are cleaning, you might be in conversation with God. It's normal for your lived-in home to need straightening up. It's normal for your lived-in body to need showering and other sorts of upkeep. It's normal for clothing to turn into laundry. What about your heart and soul?

In God's presence, look at your soul. Straighten up what is a bit out of place. Clean what might be dusty—or dirty. It might not stay clean for long. But for now, things are fine.

Be pleased together—you and God—with the results!

29

ON THE STREET

As you go down the street (walking, driving, biking, roller-blading)
or ride the bus or train,
look at the people along the way.

While waiting at a checkout line
or in a doctor's office,
look at the people.
Look at them carefully (discreetly, of course).
Be—with God—in the presence of these people.
Pray for them.

If you are walking in a busy area,
silently bless each person or group you pass.
Silently bless the people on the bus or train or plane with you.
Ask God to give them what they need.
Thank God for them and for yourself.
Be quiet for a bit in your God's presence.

30

WRAPPING GIFTS

When do you wrap gifts? Christmas, birthdays, weddings, graduations, times of need?

Don't you wrap gifts when you want to pay special attention to someone?

While wrapping the gift, let your mind and heart be occupied with the person and the event that occasions the gift.

Hold the person in your heart. Look, with God, at the person. And, together with God, love this person.

You are giving this gift. Thank God for the gift of this person's life.

You can perhaps ask God to give the person what God wants to give. That, you can be sure, will always be the best gift—and one of which you are a part.

31

BEDTIME

When you finally have your children ready for bed, what do you do (besides thank God it is bedtime!)?

~ Do you read them a story?
~ Do you allow one last drink of water?
~ Do you say "night prayers" with them?

Might you pray together? Go over the day (maybe each of you can do that quietly; you have had different days or different reactions to the same day). Ask God to bless the people of the day. Say you're sorry for any part you played in the day that wasn't good. Ask for help for the next day.

Then pause together and spend a few moments just enjoying God's love for you. You can count on it! God loves you, without condition, every moment of your life.

With a last gesture (hug, pat, kiss, blanket, tuck), whisper to your children that you love them very much.

As much as you love them, God loves them more! Bask in God's love for all of you!

PRAYER THAT WORSHIPS

32

ADORATION

Take time to think about everything you know about God (not Jesus, GOD). Think about one thing at a time. For instance:

~ God always is; God has no beginning, no end.
~ God creates everything that is (the cosmos and all that's in it!).
~ God creates everyone who is (who ever was and is to come!).
~ God keeps everything and everyone in existence.
~ God knows everything about you (and about everyone else).
~ God loves you unconditionally.

The list can go on and on. If it is God you think about, you cannot really wrap your mind around it: God is too great!

Get lost in your contemplation of God. Adore, praise, and be in wonder of God.

Be with your God, wherever your prayer takes you.

33

BEAUTY

Think about when you hear yourself saying, "Isn't that beautiful!" or just, "Beautiful!" You might say that about a child, a scene, an accomplishment, a song. Whatever it is, when you experience it, you are full of delight because it is indeed beautiful. There's a radiance in it, a harmony, the sight or sound or feel of which fills you with delight.

Take a moment to be conscious that God is present to you. Now be aware of someone or something that is beautiful. Look, listen, touch (right now in the physical world or in your memory or imagination). Let the beauty of it give you pleasure.

Remember how the poet Hopkins wrote of God: "He who fathers forth all beauty."

Let the beauty you enjoy move you to the One who *is* beauty. Delight in God. Let your delight turn to praising God.

Then delight some more.

34

GIVING GLORY

How do you give God glory? Do you sing about it in church? exclaim about it when moved?

What about *doing* it?

~ When you do something well, remember God and give glory.
~ When you say something well, remember God and give glory.
~ When you make something well, remember God and give glory.

Take a moment, if you will. Think back over the day.

~ What did you do well?
~ What did you say well?
~ What did you make well?

Whether or not someone noticed or remarked on it or thanked you, what was it you did or said or made well?

Give God glory!

35

MAKING MUSIC

If you play a guitar, strum the strings. (You can adapt this to any instrument.)
Strum the strings until you fall into patterns.
When you settle into the pleasing tones,
let your mind and heart be quiet.
Fall into the music you are making.
Fall into the presence of the God who created you.
Be conscious of the God who helps you create.
Let the music help you sustain this prayer.

If the music should fade or stumble, let it. Remain with your God.

36

LISTENING TO MUSIC

If you love opera (or other music), listen to some.
While listening, do not do anything else.
Give yourself to the music.
Experience being in the music.

While experiencing the music, be aware of God.
Do nothing else.
Give yourself to God.
Experience being in God.
Be aware only of your God.

37

MUTE

You can be mute when you are experiencing God's presence:
your all-holy God
(Reflect on what that means to you.)
your God who is your very life
(Reflect on what that means to you.)
your God who is love
(Reflect on what that means to you.)

You can be mute—
and in your silence
with every aspect of your being
worship God.

38

LOVE SONGS

Have you a favorite love song?

Do you know a love song? It could be something on the charts now, an "oldie but goodie," a classical piece—it makes no difference as long as it expresses your love.

Do you remember the music? the lyrics?

If you do, then in the privacy of your car, at home (if you can manage it), or in your mind (that works with God), sing your favorite love song to the Lord.

Sing the words that express your love best, singing them over and over. God doesn't get tired of them.

Bask in your love for God.

Bask in God's love for you.

If you have a favorite love poem, proclaim that love poem to your God. Or, like a little child, make up your own tunes. Make happy sounds, a "joyful noise" to sing your love.

39

CELEBRATION

People sometimes wonder who they are. Articles, workshops, and conversations might help in this discovery. But there is a simple and prayerful way to come to the truth of who you are.

In the presence of your God, look at what you have given in the past week (or month or whatever time frame suits you).

~ *What* have you given?
~ To *whom* have you given?
~ *Why* have you given?
~ *How* have you given? (How involved was your heart in the giving?)

Giving is cause for celebration. In giving, you celebrate *you*—who you are. In giving, you also celebrate your God—who first gave you your true self.

As you think about celebration—of yourself, of God—how does your heart want to pray?

40

THOUGHT-LESS

When you are doing something you enjoy doing, concentration generally comes easily, doesn't it?

Think about what you like doing so much that you can say, "I get lost in it." (Gardening? Listening to music? Looking at a new baby?)

The next time you start to do this, begin by asking God to be with you. Even as you are not thinking, but thoroughly immersed in your task, God is with you. Ask God to remind you, nudge you, move you—when you are about finished—to segue into prayer.

As you finish (maybe before you clean up and put things away or wash up or change your clothes), pause. Move a bit deeper into the internal silence you have. In that silence, just be with your God.

In case you don't know already, you will find out when you pray this way why it is so very good!

41

WHO LOVES BETTER?

If—with all you are and all you have—you love God,
if you love God with all your heart and soul and mind and strength,
that is very good.

God—with all that God is—
loves you unconditionally,
ever and always.
That you exist proves it.
That you continue to exist proves it.
You so totally depend on God for your existence, for your very life.

In your prayer today
think about these things.
Let yourself realize them more deeply.

And then
respond to your great God
as you are moved.

42

HYMNS

At family prayer, at odd times during the day, at bedtime, try singing a hymn that you and your family really like.

Sing together. Let one sing while the other hums. Let one recite the lyrics you like the best. Appreciate the meaning of the words. Enjoy the poetry of the hymn. Then sing it again.

You can sing-pray at home, in the car, or on a walk.

At bedtime, hearing the familiar music and words is a lovely way to drift off to sleep. And just maybe a reluctant child will fall asleep humming—more and more slowly.

43

WHO STARTED IT?

You might say, "I began to pray and . . ." or "When I started to pray . . ."

Yes. There is a time when you started to pray. But was that the prayer's beginning? No.

Every prayer is a response to an invitation—God's. God always starts it. (It's safe to blame God for this!)

In your prayer, thank God for the invitation to be together. Thank God even more by enjoying your relationship.

Maybe you could ask God to make you more aware of these invitations.

44

SINGING

Singing, they say, is praying twice.

As you are driving, showering, vacuuming, folding laundry, doing odd jobs—when you feel like it—sing.

The time of year doesn't matter. If you like Christmas carols and a particular carol suits your mood in April—sing it.

If there is a hymn that comes to your mind or expresses how you feel this day—sing it.

If there is another song that articulates what you are going through, how you feel, what you hope for—sing it.

If there's a piece of music you just plain like—sing it (or hum it or "make a joyful noise," as your voice allows).

Sing it *to* your God. Sing it *for* your God. Sing it *with* the joy of living to the God who makes you alive!

45

WHEN AT FAULT

You are still aware of the fault in you that, try as you might, keeps plaguing you. Good intentions notwithstanding, that fault is there, in your life. Maybe not all the time, but it's there.

Perhaps you are saying, "It is beyond me to do any better with this." Maybe it is. Maybe with God's grace it isn't. But right now things are not as good in you as you would like.

Let God know about this fault (God already knows, but tell God anyway). Tell God what is in your heart.

Then let yourself think about God:
~ God who is all-holy,
~ God who is all-good,
~ God who is all-loving.

Lose yourself in awe and wonder of God. This puts the fault in perspective.

Allow that fault to lead you to adoration of your God.

46

ALONE

Many people are disappointed in their friendships or in their marriages. Sometimes we discover that our expectations are too high. When some sort of test comes (you might have thought it an ordinary event and not a test), the other person fails you. Matters that you expected to be taken care of are left unattended. What's worse is that the other person is surprised that you are displeased. This surprise might be more painful to you than the initial offense.

Time and time again you might realize that someone does not know you or love you as well as you thought. Will you always be this alone? Will no one ever really know you or care for you?

Do you know *yourself* so well that you never surprise yourself? never change or grow? By now you should know that you are a mystery that possibly no other person—even you—can know.

No one can know you thoroughly—on every level, at all times—except the God who created you. Nor can anyone love you thoroughly except God. Only your Creator can know and love you as you are at every moment because only God is working in you—creating you—at every moment.

There is something sacred about the truth that only God can be in the very depths of your being, knowing and loving you, for always. How might you respond?

PRAYER WITH THE BODY

47

BREATHING

You want to pray. You have made time for prayer. You are *ready!*

Maybe you can't get started. You ask God for help. What comes to mind are all the things you still have to do. God doesn't seem to be paying much attention. Would God notice if you tied ribbons to your halo? Should you keep torturing yourself?

Torture? No! Jesus said, "I have come to bring *life* and *life* to the fullest" (see John 10:10). Prayer wasn't meant to be torture. There is a perfectly natural way to quiet down, and it doesn't cost money. It's called breathing.

Breathe so slowly and so rhythmically that you cannot think of anything else. If you have a second hand on your watch, it might help to look at it.

Breathe in for five seconds.

Hold the breath for five seconds.

Breathe out for five seconds.

Wait five seconds before taking another breath.

Until you are used to it, you are likely to lose the rhythm here and there. That's expected. Just start again.

Usually it takes two or three tries at this exercise for your mind to empty. Let your thoughts drift back to a small part of a Scripture passage. Continue breathing slowly, but not so slowly as to be distracting.

Sometimes prayer needs to be wooed.

48

COUNTDOWN TO ZERO

One often hears, "Count to ten before you speak."
If it works for you, do it.
If you need something else, try this:
Start with ten.
Let your body feel all the tension of ten.
Go to nine.
Let your body feel nine.
Go to eight.
Feel your body relaxing to eight.
Continue down, number by number,
feeling your way while
counting to zero.
Take your time.
Hold it at zero.
Hold it a bit longer at zero.
See what God does.

49

WORSHIP DANCE

Play a favorite tape or CD, preferably one that suits your mood (or a mood you wish you were in!).

Dance with the music as you wish, as you can,
for as long as it pleases you.
Be aware of your body and its abilities,
and thank God for your body.
Be aware of the music and your body,
using both in a single act of—
worship? praise? thanksgiving?
Some days, your dance may dance you
into the arms of God.
Be with God in your dance.

50

DANCING (WITH OR WITHOUT MUSIC)

Lie on the floor.
Stretch, relax.
Hear the music—externally or in your mind or both.
Let your body, part by part, respond to the music.
Surrender to the music.
Know the rightness of your body's surrender.

In the quiet that follows, think of your God.
And surrender to God—
as simply, as rightly as your body surrenders to music.
In this surrender to your God,
worship.

51

EXERCISING

Do this while walking, jogging, cycling, using machines, or engaging in any kind of exercise. Once you find the pattern and establish the rhythm of the exercise, be conscious of the parts of your body working—and working together.

Enjoy the health that allows you to exercise.
As you think about each working part of your body, thank God for it.
As you think about all parts working together, thank God for that.
Think about the people and parts of your life. Thank God for them.
Think about all the people and parts of your life working together. Thank God for that.
If there is some part or person that is making noise and interfering with everything working smoothly, pay attention. (Pay attention, too, if something is downright disruptive.)
In God's presence, pay attention.
Let your prayer take you where your life needs to be.

52

HANDS

Look at your hands.

List the ways you have used your hands since first waking this morning. (It's probably a long list!) If you want, think of other ways you use your hands. Thank God for the use of these hands.

If you are willing, think of other people's hands. There are the close-by hands of friends or those in your household or workplace. At whose hands do you suffer? benefit? Let God know.

The Bible mentions hands 1,059 times! "Your hand" is written 150 times. Whether "your hand" is prayed ("Stretch forth your hand, O God," followed by a petition) or is applied to a person ("done by your hand"), "hand" seems to be a way of naming the person who is doing something.

Look, with God, at your hands. Consider, with God, not only the things your hands do, but also the way you use your hands.

Are your hands loving when they touch, or punishing? Are they indifferent? selfish? generous?

How are your hands?

How are you?

As God holds your hands, how does your heart want to pray?

53

CANDLES

A lighted candle (scented or not—it's your preference) provides a lovely, helpful focus for praying. If it is dark, you might make it the only light in the room.

Gently, unhurriedly, gaze at it.

Notice the color, the shape, the movement of the flame. Attend to the center of the flame. Be aware of the sight and scent of it. Then . . .

Wonder (being conscious of God's presence) about the flame at the center of your life, whatever it is that gives you life.

Wonder about Jesus' statement "I am the light of the world" (John 8:12). What effect do you want his claim to have on the way you treat others? on the way you live?

Pray to God as your heart moves you.

54

STEPPING INTO THE DAY

Do this when you first wake up in the morning, when you first get out of bed.

Get up slowly and deliberately.
Take one step, praying, *God, you give me this day. I step into it.*
(Pause, reflecting on this, as long as you like.)
Take a second step, praying, *God, you give me myself. I take into this day the self you have given me.*
(Pause, reflecting on this, as long as you like.)
Take a third step, praying, *God, you and your ways are often mysterious. I step into the mystery of this day, trusting you and your love for me.*
(Pause, reflecting on this, as long as you like.)
Take a fourth step, ending this prayer. Perhaps use the Sign of the Cross, the Lord's Prayer, the Glory Be, or another prayer.

55

SLEEP

"It's time to go to bed." You say this to your children, your spouse, even yourself. When it's time, you want to sleep. If sleep doesn't come, you toss and turn and maybe complain. In the morning, someone might ask, "Did you sleep well?"

What happens when you sleep? Well, your body gets rest. Your body might need to heal, and sleep facilitates that. Sometimes sleep helps you forget things. It also brings you closer to tomorrow.

What else?

Most of the time you give yourself to sleep; it's something you welcome. To do that you have to surrender—to sleep and to the unconsciousness it brings. Be vulnerable to sleep and sleeping time. Sleep is natural. It should be a daily occurrence.

You might ask yourself, *How is it that, generally speaking, I surrender to sleep gladly? (Easy!) How is it that I find it difficult to surrender to God—no matter what—even though I know that God loves me?*

Thinking about this—and conversing with God about it—can be very good prayer.

56

SWIMMING

When swimming laps, let your mind and body be immersed in the rhythm of it.

You might be aware of the water and your body.

Be aware of the living water and your being.

Be aware of the One
in whom you
"live and move and have [your] being" (Acts 17:28).

Be with God in your swimming.

57

HERE AND NOW

A person can be present to you physically, here and now. Such presence may be welcome or unwelcome or neutral. When a person you welcome is present to you by attending to you, mind and heart, you experience the kind of presence that this prayer brings.

Take several deep, slow breaths.
Become as still in your person as you can be.
Let yourself muse on these facts:
You, in your very being,
come from the mystery who is God.
You, in your very being,
will return to the mystery who is God.
After spending a few moments with this awesome reality, ask yourself, *What, truly, is the greatest privilege I can experience in my lifetime?* Think long and hard and maybe several times over.
Might the greatest privilege be to live in the presence of God?
For God is with you always, in every here and now.

58

YOUR BODY

You probably know well the greatest commandment: to love the Lord your God with your whole mind, your whole heart, your whole strength—in other words, with all you are and all you have.

One of the ways to express this kind of love is by using your body in prayer. Think about what you are saying to your God. Reinforce it with your body language. (Watch children. When they want something, when they don't want to do something, or when they are afraid, their bodies reflect their feelings!)

You are God's much-loved and cherished child. You can be entirely yourself. God knows *you*, so there's no surprise or embarrassing reaction on God's part, whether you

~ want something: "Please! Please! Please!"

~ are sorry about something: "I am so sorry. If you will only look at my heart, you will see it."

~ yearn for God: "Come, Lord Jesus, come."

Some people kneel, some stand, some sit, some manage a lotus position, and some stay in bed. Use gestures or change position, as your heart dictates. Don't think about it too much; just do whatever helps you be in the presence of your God.

Once you get used to it, your prayer might take on new life. Try it!

59

READY FOR THE DAY

Mornings can be such a rush! There is so much to do and so little time in which to do it. (Not to mention what it's like for those who are not "morning people.")

Take time for several long, slow breaths. (The important thing is to do *nothing* else while taking your long, slow breaths. And, yes, you can do this in bed before anyone else knows you're awake.)

During the longest, slowest breath you can manage, attend only to your breath.

During the second breath, let yourself be conscious that your day is beginning. (But don't start thinking about all that you have to do.)

During the third breath, remember that God is always with you, loving you.

On the fourth breath, ask God (you don't have to use words; just knowing is enough) to keep you from harm's way, to shield you from evil, to prevent you from doing or saying anything you'd be ashamed of.

For the fifth breath, ask God to have things go well for you today. Then thank God for being God.

End with another long, slow breath.

Of course, you can do whatever you want with any of your breaths. You might want to stand or kneel or gesture according to what you are breathing.

60

BUSY MIND

You need to give special attention to preparing for prayer when your mind is busy. It seems that, no matter how hard you try, your mind keeps thinking. You cannot focus on your prayer because of your chattering mind.

One way to still an unquiet mind is to make prayerful gestures—a kind of holy exercising. Use your body to prepare your mind for prayer.

Make the Sign of the Cross. Unite your spirit with God: Father, Son, Spirit.

Genuflect. In the exercise of standing, kneeling on one knee, pausing to ask God to bring you consciously into the Holy Presence, and standing again, you are using your body to pray. Make the Sign of the Cross again. Pause.

Raise your arms in supplication to your God. Let your raised arms be expressive of your yearning to be in communion with the Holy One.

Extend your arms in the form of a cross. Unite your spirit with Jesus.

Kneel. Kneeling reminds you of how great God is and how safe you are before your God.

Make these gestures, or others of your choice, repeatedly until your prayer flows.

PRAYER WITH THE MIND

61

GOSPEL STORIES

When reading a Gospel story, look at the people mentioned in it. Decide which one you want to be (you can be a main character or an onlooker). Reread the story, seeing yourself as (and feeling like) a participant.

Now, how do you want to have a conversation with Jesus? Tell him how you see the situation and how it might relate to something in your life. Let Jesus know what this Gospel story means to you.

Pause. Listen with your heart for what Jesus might want to say to you. Respond.

Ask for help—as you see the need, as he sees the need.

Go back into the Gospel story and read it prayerfully once more.

End your prayer in a way that suits you and your relationship with Jesus.

62

NAMES

Think of your favorite name for God. You may, at this time in your life, be attracted to names such as God the Father, Abba, Jesus, Lord, Spirit, Consoler. You may have a private, intimate way of calling God. It might be as simple as "O God" or "my or God" or "Himself." Think of your way of naming God (or how you might like to name God).

Begin breathing that name. Find a slow, comfortable rhythm for saying, "Jesus . . . Jesus . . . Jesus" or "My Lord . . . my Lord . . . my Lord" or whatever suits your relationship.

You can do this for twenty minutes or so. If you "drift off" during it, aware of your God's presence, drift off. Pick it up again as you need to.

If you do this for a while every day and for short moments during the day (when unlocking the car or waiting for a bus or subway), you might be surprised at how this prayer will begin praying itself in you. Even during the night. You'll see.

63

NO WORDS

Sometimes
you know
what you mean.

Sometimes
you cannot find a way
to *say* it.

Open your mind to God.
Open your heart to God.

God knows.
God cannot misunderstand you.
God needs no explanation.

Then, with your mind open,
with your heart open,
ask God to give you
what *God* wants to give you.

And ask God to help you receive it—gladly.

64

PONDERING

When the mother of Jesus heard from the shepherds about her child, and when her lost young son was found but then asked why she searched for him, Mary pondered these things in her heart (see Luke 2:19, 51).

When things (astounding, troubling, worrisome, frightening, happy, angering) happen, ponder them in your heart.

And, as a person does when with a lover, ponder in the presence of God, who loves you. Maybe just look at God in your pondering. Maybe shrug your heart's shoulders. Maybe laugh or scream in your heart.

When you are finished, hold your pondering heart (no matter what condition it is in) before God in trust for blessing.

That is enough for now.

65

PSALMS

The psalms are great reading for prayer. (Reading for prayer is not reading for academic knowledge; it is reading to have the heart stirred and moved to good.) In the grand scope of the psalms, there is no human emotion not brought to prayer.

As you read, be aware of what the text means and what it might mean for you. When something strikes your heart, pause. Let your mind and heart be with it. (Maybe you will think, maybe not. Just *be* with the sacred words.)

Perhaps you'll want to memorize a line or two. If you do, repeat that phrase often during the day, letting its meaning sink into you. If it's one that affects you deeply, you might want to stay with it a few days—or weeks—or make it a part of your life.

Sacred words have a way of becoming alive in you, if you allow them to.

66

QUESTIONS

In the Gospel stories Jesus asks questions.
Once Jesus asked his disciples,
"Who do people say I am?"
They told him.
Then he continued,
"Who do *you* say I am?"
In your imagination, see yourself in that group.
Hear Jesus say your name while looking you in the eye.
Hear Jesus ask *you*,
"Who do you say I am?"
Take your time answering him.
Later, if you wish, you might ask Jesus,
"Who do you say *I* am?"

67

QUESTIONS AGAIN

Imagine yourself in a crowd, listening to Jesus. Hear Jesus asking one of the people, "What do you want?"

See Jesus turning to you and asking, "What do you want?" (Remember, it is *Jesus* asking *you* what he can do for you!)

Answer him.

Then, true to the gospel, Jesus is likely to ask, "Do you believe?"

Answer him again.

Wait. Be aware of Jesus being with you during this prayer.

68

DID . . . DIDN'T

Read a Gospel story in which Jesus interacts with people like Zacchaeus, the woman at the well, or the woman caught in adultery.

Read it again.

Then make a list (mentally is fine) of what Jesus did.

Make another list of what Jesus didn't do.

Really think about it. (It's fun to do this with another person, perhaps someone in your family. Children generally are very good at it.)

Being conscious of God's presence with you, mull over what Jesus did and didn't do.

Reflect on where your attitude or actions might be different from those of Jesus.

What do you want to ask of your God?

69

GLASSES

Those who did not grow up wearing glasses generally find that it takes some time to get used to them—
to remember to put them on
to remember where you left them
to wonder if your eyes are getting worse
(until someone remarks on how smudged your glasses are!).

But, oh!
Things are so much clearer,
give more pleasure,
and reveal more detail.
Glasses *are* worth the trouble.

Scripture tells us to put on the mind of Christ.
To see other people, situations, and the world
with the eyes of Christ.

When you think about your day with your God,
look at it with your eyes, your mind;
try to look at it with the eyes, the mind, of Christ.

Take the trouble!
People will be much more lovable.
You will be more peaceful.

When you think about it,
how does your heart want to pray?

70

I DON'T UNDERSTAND

The assumption is that we *should* understand.
That's what we desire.
We want to know *why*.
If we know why,
then maybe we can do something about it—
or at least be better at living with it.

Life isn't like that.
There is much we do not (maybe cannot) understand.

Tell God about it.
Ask God, if it is good for you (or someone else),
to help you understand.
Or not.
Because, sometimes,
not understanding,
living in the mystery of it,
in your God's ever-loving presence,
might be the sun and the rain
of your coming to flower and fruit.

Trust your God.
And if that is too hard right now,
pray the prayer of the child's father:
I believe; help my unbelief! (Mark 9:24).

71

STORIES

When children listen to stories, they turn inward, identifying with characters, guessing the next part.
Their eyes reveal some of what is going on in their hearts and minds.
Adults are, at heart, no different.
Would you pick a Bible story for yourself today?
Listen to it as a child might.
Turn inward, identifying with the people in it.
Feel it for yourself.
Wonder about it.
Let the eyes of your heart look at God deep within,
knowing that God sees you with love.
Tell God how you understand the story,
what the story means to you.
Listen with your heart.
End this prayer time thanking and praising God
or doing whatever your heart desires.

72

ONLY

Take time (in God's presence, of course) to think of all the things you can do. Limit yourself by naming the things that *only* you can do. Pretty amazing, isn't it?

As with the woman at the well, let your Lord tell you about all that you have ever done and all that only you can do. Take your time as you do this.

Now turn the tables. Take time to think of those things that only God can be, that *only* God can do. (Ask God to help you make the list as good and as long as you can.)

Let the meaning of that list of what only God can be, *only* God can do, get through to you.

How does thinking about this affect you?

Pray your soul's response!

73

IMAGINATION

Imagination is part of the normal equipment of every human brain. No human intellect can function without it. Of course, some people have stronger or better-developed imaginations than others. But if you worry or can make plans, your imagination is in good shape.

Go, in your imagination, to a place where you like to be. Take a few moments to enjoy being there.

Notice someone coming. As he comes closer, you *know* it is Jesus. When he comes up to you, greet each other. Now walk or sit together for a while, enjoying each other and this place.

See Jesus turn to you and look you in the face. Hear him say your name. Hear the question he puts to you.

(You can use questions Jesus asked in the Gospels: "Do you love me?" "Do you believe?" "What do you want?" "Who do you say that I am?" "Will you also go away?" * There are dozens more. Take your pick.)

Answer Jesus. In words, if you want. Open your mind and heart to him, if you so choose. Spend time together.

Later you might want to ask Jesus the same question about yourself!

*These questions are found in John 21:16, Matthew 9:28, Matthew 20:21, Mark 8:29, and John 6:67 (JB) respectively.

74

THIS DAY

Any Gospel text will do. What is preferable is the Scripture passage for the day. You can find it in the readings of the day (your church bulletin might carry it), the Liturgy of the Hours, or one of the little books of Scripture readings. If you want, you can begin praying the Sunday readings the week before.

One of the pleasures of doing this is knowing that Christians (at least those who use a lectionary) all over the world are praying from the same text as you. It's a great experience of community.

Read the text. Ask yourself, *In light of this text, where do I see God active in my life this day? For what grace might I ask?*

If you do this early in the day, go back to it in the evening. Once again ask yourself, *Where do I see God as having been active in my life this day? Was I aware of it? Did it affect the way I spoke or acted?*

What from this day do you want to bring before the face of God?

75

BAGGAGE

When you go to prayer, there are probably times when your mind goes and goes and goes. You want to pray. You want to focus. But your mind seems to have a mind of its own and won't let you be quiet.

When it happens, you can try this:

Take a deep breath or two.

In your imagination see, one at a time, all of the things that are on your mind. Take each one (making dinner, attending a meeting, taking a child to soccer practice, finishing a report) and put it into its own suitcase.

Take as long as you need to get it all packed.
Look at your pile of luggage.
Check it.
Take the baggage check with you, safely stowed in a pocket or purse.
You know it's safe. You can claim it at will.
Now go back to your prayer.

PRAYER IN SUFFERING

76

HURTING FOR OTHERS

It's bad enough when *you* are hurt so badly that you hate another person. But when someone you love dearly is harmed, your hatred can reach a new ferocity. If this is true of you, it will take a stronger effort of your soul to prevent that hatred from harming you.

How do you pray?

Jesus' mother might be a good person to approach. Look how people talked about and treated her son. Look how they tried to trap him. Then came his arrest, passion, and death.

Jesus, the Lamb of God. Jesus, the innocent one. Jesus, Mary's son.

According to tradition, Mary saw Jesus on the road to Calvary. In John's Gospel Mary stood at the foot of the cross watching her son die, unable to take care of him. Later she held his lifeless body. As a widow, as a mother of an only and innocent adult child, how do you think she felt? Take time to ponder that.

Ask Mary, the mother of Jesus, to be with you. Ask her to help you come through this suffering as she did hers. Come, with Mary's intercession, to a deeper level of your graced humanity—a level at which you can truly let your hatred dissolve. Then you can forgive and be whole again.

Jesus did it. Mary did it. With the help of the Father of all, so can you. Pray with all your heart for this to be so.

77

MANAGED CARE

Getting the best affordable health care these days often demands complicated decision making. Results can be frustrating and frightening.

In God's presence (and maybe also with a family member or friend or adviser) sort through your assumptions and expectations. What did you expect your coverage to supply? Were you ignorant? What are the facts of managed care?

Ask God for help in understanding the reality of the situation. Ask for help in knowing yourself—your frustration and anger, your financial fears, your difficulty in facing up to this reality. Take your time. Remember that Jesus said, "I am the way, and the *truth*, and the life" (John 14:6, italics mine). Truth is important here. On a deeper level, so is understanding.

Ask your God for help in knowing the wisest thing for you to do. How can you, under the circumstances, best arrange for health care? How can you manage managed care in your situation? To whom can you go for advice?

How can your spirit remain peaceful during this time?

Ask God about being peaceful.

Listen.

Give God time to answer you in God's way. (Don't be surprised if God's way is surprising.)

78

DIRTY HANDS

You know what is right; you know what you stand for. Integrity (your personal integrity) is most valuable to you. You intend to keep it.

The question is, in this situation, how do you do it?

How can you be effective in the here and now? Especially when (in your judgment) others are playing dirty? You are accosted by half-truths and twisted truths. If they were outright lies, you could deny them. These partial truths, these selective statements, are what make you so frustrated.

How do you defend yourself without dirtying your hands? How do you let go without dirtying your hands?

How do you have the wisdom to know whether to fight or to remove yourself from the encounter (at least in your mind and heart)?

Here is a time when you can immerse yourself (with God's help, but God always helps!) in God the Holy

Spirit. With a sincere and open heart, beg the Holy Spirit to give you wisdom. Beg the Holy Spirit to help you speak and act in a way that will harm no one (starting with you). While you are doing this, also beg the Holy Spirit to help you hear God's Word and not turn away.

This is not always easy to do. But it is always worth it. (And you won't have dirty hands!)

79

EMPTY

Every so often (and for too long a time, it seems) you might feel empty. Nothing there. Nothing worth getting up for. "What difference do I make?" "Why bother?" "Who cares?" are the questions that haunt you.

It's hardly the most cheerful time of your life, but it doesn't have to be useless.

Show God your empty heart. Show God your discouraged mind. Be aware, with God, of your listlessness. Flood God (as best you can) with your misery.

If you are up to it, invite God to your private pity party. Wallow in your spirit's lack of energy.

When you get tired of this (or just don't care), ask God to fill your emptiness with the gift God wants to give you.

Appeal to God for trust and patience. And rest content, remembering that God has a different time line. God never fails.

80

WHEN THINGS DON'T WORK OUT

Things don't always work out. It might be your fault or somebody else's. It might be circumstances. But something did not work out.

How might you pray?

You might think of the sufferings of Jesus. He wept over the people of Jerusalem because they *rejected* him. Sometimes he was sad because his apostles *didn't understand* him. One of his closest friends *betrayed* him—for money. Another close friend *swore he didn't even know* him! His arrest and crucifixion must have looked like great failure to people. Yet through Jesus' suffering came his resurrection and our salvation.

Go to Jesus. (Remember, some say that being rejected, betrayed, denied, and misunderstood caused him more pain than being crucified!) Unite your sufferings with his. That won't take your suffering away. But it just might bring you closer to your God.

81

ACCUSATIONS

What you do (or don't do) makes sense to you. (That is true of everyone, even though what others do might not always make sense to you.)

You know why you do (or don't do) what you do. At least some of the time. Others might misunderstand you, accuse you of intentions you never had, blame you for things that never crossed your mind.

When you get over the surprise of the accusation, take time to be conscious of your God's being with you. Go over the situation with God (using your mind, heart, feelings, and judgment). Be quiet a bit. Do it again. When something strikes you, go back to it. When you want to rush by some aspect of the accusation, go back to it.

God is truth. God knows about the situation anyway; you are utterly safe exploring it with your God. More likely than not you are dealing with a jumble of things. Some you can identify. Some you can't.

Ask God's help in accomplishing what you can do something about. Leave in God's hands what you cannot do anything about.

There really is nothing else to do—if you live well.

82

THE JOB

Downsizing.

Two out of five must go.

You don't have seniority.

Jobs in your area are scarce.

If you were to write down everything you feel, you'd fill pages.

How do you come to your God in prayer?

The first round might be fear, anger, embarrassment, panic, anxiety, despair. Perhaps you rage against God, reminding God of the word *providence*. You ride your own emotional roller coaster. (And while you're riding it, you may well be reassuring your children or other dependents with a confidence you don't feel.)

Why not take God with you on your emotional roller-coaster ride? Why not show God the turmoil of your very full heart, the sleeplessness of your nights, the difficulty of the unemployment line, the pressure of overdue bills?

Of course you are begging God to help you find work. You are working at finding work. Show God your discouragement.

While you continue searching for employment, ask God also for the faith to pray, *Give me what you want to give me. Let me and my family learn from this what you want us to learn and become the people you want us to become.*

Probably only hindsight will show you how wondrously that prayer gets answered.

83

CHAFF

"Why me?" you might ask. "What did I do that God is punishing me like this?" When bad things happen to good people, maybe you ask, "Why should that happen to them? They don't deserve it!"

It's not likely that God is "punishing" you or them. The *why* of suffering is often a mystery. Sometimes all you can do—gracefully—is to surrender in trust. Imitate Jesus in the Garden of Gethsemane.

There is an analogy in the life cycle of wheat. Wheat grows with a husk around the kernel. Some people call this husk, or chaff, useless. In the process of harvesting, wheat is threshed or winnowed. The husks are removed and discarded. If the husk is removed before the wheat ripens, the wheat will not mature. It cannot become food. It will wither, incomplete.

Perhaps the circumstances of your life that are unfair, frustrating, or painful could be considered chaff. They function as a vital part of your spiritual growth.

When you "ripen," the chaff can be threshed away. Only God knows the right time for that. Inevitably the result is a more grace-filled you, with a fuller, better life.

In this meantime, how does your heart want to pray?

84

BETRAYAL

Are there many ways of suffering worse than being betrayed? Whether the betrayal is by a spouse, another family member, a friend, or someone at work (each situation with its own nuance), the anguish of betrayal can overwhelm you.

Your first reaction is likely to be disbelief. You simply do not believe that this is happening to you. Questions follow disbelief: *Why? What did I do? How could they?* Your suffering is all but unbearable.

How do you take care of yourself—especially your spirit—at a time like this?

Thank God if you have loving people to be with you during this time. It helps, but it isn't enough. You can't help wanting more.

Maybe you need to wail for a while. If so, what about doing it with God? It's safe, you know. Besides, Jesus had Judas to contend with. Jesus knows what betrayal is like. (For heaven's sake, don't short-circuit your pain by saying something like "Well, my case is nothing compared to what Jesus suffered." Don't bother comparing.) Don't try to dismiss your suffering before God. This is your suffering NOW. How else can you honestly go to your God with it other than however you are? (In the psalms you'll find some first-class wailing! There's good company for you in the psalms.)

Hold your angry, shredded, vengeful, despairing, hateful, wronged, broken self before God. Ask God to look at you and to heal you with that look. Ask for the grace to accept the healing that God will (eventually) make real in you.

85

SUFFERING

Suffering is a part of every human life. Suffering is the part of life that places you at a fork in the road. How do you behave when things are not of your liking or under your control? How do you let it affect you and the people around you?

When you are experiencing hard times, take a moment to recognize that God is with you. With God at your side, look at that part of your life that is not under your control—a person, a circumstance about which you can do nothing. You suffer from it.

Things are not going the way you think they should be going. Hard times come from physical illness or disability, emotional pain, disrupted or poor relationships, dissatisfaction in family or work or social life, losses in life. It's hard. You suffer. You cry out, "It's not fair!" You are right.

Things made of parts fall apart. Nature takes its course. People are free and limited, are intelligent and foolish, are loving and not so loving. They fall short of what they should be. When this happens, everyone suffers.

The important question is, what are you going to do about it? How might you use suffering for your own (and others') good? As you undergo injustice, endure pain, live through hard times, how are you in your inmost self? Look not only at the circumstance but also at how you are handling it. How are you living this experience? How are other people affected by it?

Suffering can make or break you. You can use it to become more compassionate or more cynical or more apathetic.

Ask God for what you need. As you think about it, ask God to heal you where you have been wounded.

Please, don't give up. And, please, don't be unaware of what God is giving you. Always rest secure in God's faithful love for you.

86

EXPECTATIONS

Always and ever people have expectations of you. You might not know about some of them. Suddenly one day you find yourself in trouble for not having lived up to someone's expectations of you.

Probably every child in the world knows this. Maybe the child was ignorant of the expectation. Maybe it was forgotten. Maybe it was beyond the child, for whatever reason, at that time. When parents, family members, teachers, or other children don't have their expectations (reasonable or not) met, generally the child suffers in some way. How does a child deal with this?

Children have no monopoly on not meeting expectations. Spouses don't; relatives don't; friends don't; neighbors and coworkers don't. How do you suffer this situation?

Many people, starting as suffering children, try to adapt to others' expectations. Wanting approval, wanting to please, they accommodate. At times this is a good thing to do. At times it is not. How do you know the difference?

Jesus says, "You will know them by their fruits" (Matthew 7:20).

Go to God in the depths of your soul. Let God know the situation from you. Ask God what God's expectations of you are. God knows you; God wants your good. God always helps you to meet God's expectations.

This suffering brings you to God in another way. Will you be true to God's image of you or someone else's? Will you suffer what you must to be your authentic self, or will you suffer being an undue people pleaser? It's your choice.

Be sure to make it, honestly, prayerfully, in your God's presence.

87

INVISIBLE

You are a certain height. You have a certain weight. You occupy space. You most definitely *are*.

Yet there is someone in your life who has the uncanny ability to render you invisible. It is as if you are not there at all.

The conversation flows in your presence, but as if you are not there.

Decisions that affect you are made. You are not part of the discussion. You might not even be told about the decision. Discovering it is a shock—and an embarrassing one at that.

You are unseen, unheard, unattended.

When you try to be noticed (for something other than being of service), you are punished for it in some demeaning or cruel way.

This is a time for some serious thinking and praying.

What is happening? It might be ignorance or insensitivity on the other person's part. It is an offense against you, but not a malicious one. It might be one that is annoying at times, but bearable. Decide if you can suffer it without harm. It might be a deeper problem—one that you cannot change. If that's the case, find the help you need, and take care of yourself.

Through all of this suffering, be in close touch with God. Ask God to help you see the situation realistically. Tell God (if you mean it!) that you want to know your part in the situation, that you want to be of help to the other person and your relationship. Let God know that you want to "have life, and have it abundantly" (John 10:10).

Then, confident in God's love, do what is best for you and for all concerned. (Maybe you will make a mistake. Ask God's help to fix it, learn from it, and live!)

88

DYING

It's not a bad thing to think about dying.

Dying can include pain, pain control; full use of faculties, diminished use of faculties; loved ones around or not. The time to get ready is now.

While you are well (more or less) and can think (more or less), reflect on these questions: If you were called to meet God this day, how would you want to be? How would you want God to find you at the moment of your death?

Really think about it. Ask God for help to believe in God and the power of God's grace.

God's help is always there. How will you prepare to accept it?

Perhaps you will want to pray your personal version of something like this:

"God, you know I want to be yours, now and forever. Help me persevere in faith, hope, and love. When those times come (maybe you are in the middle of a difficult situation right now) when I might leave you, please help me. Don't let me leave you. Help me know your love. Keep me safe in your love, now and forever. Amen."

PRAYER FOR OTHERS

89

NEWSPAPERS

Newspapers carry dreadful stories.

Some stories are reports of natural disasters. You can only guess what these disasters do to people who lose friends and family members. You can only guess what it all means to them and what changes are required in the life of each person. But you can know that it is heartbreaking, difficult, and stressful.

As you are reading the paper, let your heart be with God and with the people you read about. Pray for these people. Pray for the safety and well-being of the rescue workers.

Perhaps you will be moved to help in some way. At the very least, you can help by praying.

If you pray with your children or friends, you might want to include the news of the day in your prayer, asking God's help for the situation and God's blessing for the people.

90

SALESPEOPLE

Just as there are all kinds of salespeople, there are all kinds of customers.

Some salespeople like to be helpful (pushy?), and some customers like to be helped (needing a great deal of service). Other customers like to be left alone. Personalities of salespeople and customers can click with or annoy one another. You never know.

When you are shopping, you can say a quick prayer for the salesperson you encounter. Pray for him or her. (A really safe prayer is to ask God to give the person what God wants—and for the person to receive it.) God and you can have your own "code" for this kind of spontaneous, with-word-or-without prayer. It need not take more than a nanosecond.

Praying for the other person might have the side effect of making you kinder or more patient. You never know.

91

EACH PERSON

How many people do you meet in a day?

How many people do you meet often enough that you need to remember things about them?

When you awaken in the morning and have time with God, ask that, as you meet each person, you remember what is important or useful for that person. Ask this of God, and really mean it.

Then, as you meet each person, you are likely to find yourself saying, "How is your son's new job working out?" "Did you have a good time up north?" "Have you had a report on your wife's tests?"

It's all part of "love your neighbor as yourself" (Mark 12:31).

Ask God to help you remember people in this way. And in the evening, thank God for the conversations you've had—even if you ended up hearing more than you bargained for!

92

EMERGENCY

When you see the blinking lights of an emergency vehicle or hear its siren, say a prayer:

~ Pray for the rescue workers, that they may be safe.

~ Pray for the rescue workers, that they may be successful.

~ Pray for those who need help.

~ Pray for all those affected by this emergency.

You may ask God for this help simply by saying so. You may ask God, wordlessly, for this help simply by holding these unknown people before God. You may hold these people in your heart while you and your God love them.

93

COMPASSION

So many people!

So many needs!

How can you meet them all?

You can't. Your energy, your financial resources, your free time—all are limited.

How can you strike a balance between wearing yourself out trying to do everything and hardening your heart and doing nothing? It gets increasingly difficult if you live a very busy life.

If this is so for you, some of your prayers might ask God to help you be honestly generous as your time, responsibilities, means, and energy allow. Try to make good on your resolution. There is, though, another aspect to this.

Sometimes when you see someone in difficulty you have to help. It's one of those things you don't think about; you just do it. Others may call you foolish or a hero; it makes no difference. *You have to do it.* Wouldn't everybody? No. Not everybody is so moved on a particular occasion. Yet the good Samaritan was moved to do neighborly things—providing first aid, transportation, a room, food, and money—for a stranger.

If you are willing, ask God to make you alert and responsive to the movement of the Holy Spirit during this day. Therein is genuine love of God and love of neighbor.

And a good you.

94

POLITICAL CANDIDATES

We see a lot of signs along highways and on people's lawns, but we see even more of them during an election year. Candidates try to keep us mindful of them; they want our votes!

Be mindful of our need for good government, and pray for the candidates. Pray that they be enlightened, that they maintain integrity, that they look after the common good of the people.

In your petition to God, keep the good of the people and the good of the candidates in your mind and heart. Pray that wisdom—that great gift of the Holy Spirit—be given to the candidates.

May all the candidates be truly wise, aided by your prayer.

95

EMPATHY

You still struggle with overcoming a particular fault. You still, from time to time, fail. Sometimes you get discouraged. If someone chides you, you might answer (with some heat), "But I'm trying!"

Take this failure to your prayer. Take your sincere, if only somewhat successful, efforts.

Don't stop with asking for God's understanding and forgiveness.

Ask God to take your experience of trying and failing and help you apply it to other people. Only God knows how hard another person is trying to overcome a weakness, habit, or failure.

Ask God to make you, if not understanding, at least compassionate to other people with their weaknesses.

Ask God, in Jesus' name, to redeem all who fail.

96

GRAND-PARENTING

Grandparenting assumes different shapes and responses these days. Two-income families, single-parent families, and blended families all provide occasions for grandparents (who thought their child-rearing years were finished) to be actively important in raising children again.

For you, for your children, and for your grandchildren, pray.

Search your heart in your God's presence.

Before feeling trapped, before thinking yourself called upon to be a savior, in the deep honesty of your heart review the situation with God. List the pros and cons. But also explore options with your God. Take time to be quiet and listen. Perhaps ask a friend or a counselor to help you with the decision about how you will or won't be involved. Then do what you do, perhaps with certain conditions, with no strings attached. (You might need God's help with that.)

Whatever you do, keep in touch with God; ask for help in doing whatever you do with respect, love, and wisdom.

You will be working with God on this frequently. You might as well be prepared to enjoy each other!

97

DARING TO ENGAGE

It takes skill and courage to truly engage with another person.

Sometimes the best gift you can give that person is to listen. Listening is work. It is more than being able to repeat the information the person gave you. Listening is hearing what the person means and how the person feels or reacts to a situation. Listening is hearing what is behind the words in order to come more fully to the truth of the person's experience. Listening entails using ears and eyes, mind and heart.

Listening is receiving what the person entrusts to you. When you have listened, then you can pray better with and for the other person. You can pray better because both you and the other person will know that your heart is engaged.

Sometimes, in order to engage with another person, you must lock eyes and exchange dangerous information.

For instance, how do you greet someone who is newly bereaved? What do you say? Or do you add to the person's sorrow by pretending you don't see him or her?

Or what do you do when someone says to you, "I have cancer" or "I've been abandoned"? How do you respond?

It takes courage and grace to engage with people when their pain makes you so ill at ease.

Reflect on the time Jesus told the apostles that he was going to suffer and die. Do you remember Peter's spontaneous rebuke of Jesus, and Jesus' response to Peter (see Matthew 16:22–23; Mark 8:32–33)? Some things are meant to be suffered. Denial is no help. So we engage with the suffering when we come alongside to be a friend.

What help, what healing, what faith do you need from God, so that you can love your neighbor as yourself?

98

YOU AND THE NEWS

Sometimes you read in the newspaper about the terrible things people do. The Oklahoma City bombing. Any bombing. Robbery. Murder. Extortion. Kidnapping. Embezzlement. The list is dismal.

Some spiritual masters say that when you read about people accused or convicted of crimes, let that remind you of your own weaknesses. Of course you would never commit such terrible crimes. Or would you? Could you in certain circumstances? What might you do when desperately afraid or angry, when pushed beyond your limits? Is it possible for you to be thoughtless or careless? What might you do without even meaning to?

When you can see how you might (under certain circumstances) commit such a sin yourself, pray for strength. Pray for the accused sinner in the paper.

Maybe you'll want to pay more attention to the ending of the Lord's Prayer: "Lead us not into temptation, but deliver us from evil."

99

STORIES

Now that people are living longer, more people are caregivers. More people, too, visit the elderly. Some older people like to tell stories of their past. Some tell them and tell them and tell them again.

Listen not just with your mind to learn something (that will lead to boredom and maybe some ungraciousness on your part) but *with your heart* to reflect on the meaning of the stories.

Are they cheerful stories of good people? Perhaps you can reflect on the working of God in those lives. Pray for awareness of God's working in your own.

Are they grumbling, grudge-filled stories, still unresolved in the storytellers' lives? Perhaps you can reflect on what you hear and pray to your God for their (and your own) healing. God's healing goes to deep places. Pray for them and yourself to be open to that healing.

Listen with your heart. Later, talk to God again about the deeper meanings of the stories you've heard.

PRAYER IN THE PAUSES

100

UNHURRIED

For your health, pick at least one thing a day (or, if it's a big thing, one a week) and determine to do it in an unhurried way.

Maybe it would be quality time with someone you love or have responsibility for.

Maybe it would be something for yourself: taking a leisurely bath, doing your nails or hair, puttering in the garden, listening to music, riding a city bus to the end of the line and back, sitting on a bench to watch people come and go—something that gives you pleasure.

Do it unhurriedly. As the calm comes, remember that God is with you. He is Emmanuel, "God with us."

Let yourself respond to this knowledge of God's presence as your heart is so inclined. Maybe you will smile at God in your heart. Maybe you will want to tell God something. Maybe you will just be content being together. Just give it time: once a day or once a week.

101

SUNRISE

Watching morning happen is a lovely way to begin the day. If you live where you can actually see the sunrise (no impediments such as buildings in your view), watching the sunrise can be a morning prayer.

As the horizon lightens, the world wakes up.
What will this day be like for you?
Ask God's blessing on yourself.
Who will people your life this day?
Ask God's blessing on them.
What will happen to you this day?
Ask God for what you will need to live the day well.
What will happen this day to the people you love?
Ask God to grant them what they will need to live the day well.
What is in the news?
Ask God's help for all concerned.

By now the sun is probably well up! Spend another quiet moment just loving God.

102

NOISE

If you are surrounded by traffic, trains, pets, children, or conversations, you are not likely to notice the sounds—unless something is different. Ordinarily those sounds are not distracting.

Then there are the added noises. As soon as you walk in the door, something (TV, CD player, radio) gets turned on. Even though you may call it "background," something on the screen catches your eye and interest every so often, doesn't it? Your mood is affected when music is played.

If there were no electronically produced sounds where you are, what might be different? Might it affect the way you listen to other people? (Some people are distracted by background music; few can resist glancing at a flickering screen.) Of course, you can hear what another person is saying, but are you listening attentively?

When you don't listen in quiet, you just might miss God's presence—God's voice speaking from within your own depths. That's a real (and unnecessary) deprivation.

Suppose, every so often, you make a quiet nest for yourself. Attend to God's presence. Be still.

Distractions will always be with us. But if we constantly allow distractions, when do we listen? When do we see?

Every so often, slow down.

Be quiet.

Be.

It might amaze you what you will hear and see.

103

PAUSING

For whatever reason, you probably don't hesitate to use the pause button on one of your machines.

Why not pause during the days of your life?

~ Pause, and enjoy the moment: the sight, the sound, the feel of it.
~ Pause, and savor the moment: the experience, the meaning of it.
~ Pause, and acknowledge that there is something (small or large) that you wanted and now have.
~ Pause, and thank God for whatever you wish.
~ Pause, and just breathe.

A machine on pause merely pauses. A human being on pause does much more. You'll see.

104

WHO LOVES MORE?

Remember that you are in God's presence.

You love God.

Let God know *how* and *how much* you love.
Let God know what loving God means to you.

God loves you.
Let yourself know—down deep—that God loves you.
Take time to let it sink in: It is God who loves you,
God who knows you from forever,
God who knows all about you,
God!

Let yourself know—truly and deeply—that God loves you *infinitely* more than you could possibly love God.

Spend some time thinking about this.

When you are ready,
respond to God as your heart prompts you.

105

SUPPER

Supper is a time when, sometimes, you have guests. If you are hosting a meal, what do you do?

You issue the invitation, plan the menu, shop for groceries, clean the house, set the table, and prepare and serve the food. You make certain (as you can) that the children are presentable and the guests are compatible.

Is that all? Hardly.

You share home and food; you also share yourself in conversation. You talk about concerns, common interests, jokes, stories, politics, religion, or sports—and all the while you are attentive to your guests' needs. Do they prefer this or that beverage? Do their glasses need refilling? If all goes well, your friendship thrives.

Think, for a moment or two, about meals you have hosted and about how it is when guests come to your table.

Then think about your coming to the table of the Lord. Meditate on the Lord's being *your* host.

You might want to do this the next time you participate in the Eucharist. The meal itself (a morsel of bread, a sip of wine) is meager. The real feast is in the conversation—the prayer.

What kind of guest are you?

106

TAKING A WALK

In the evening, when things are relatively quiet, take a walk alone.

As you stroll (or power-walk, if you can think while doing that), go over your day.

In the presence of your God, replay the day. Look at the people in it, the conversations, the interactions. Examine your decisions. Review the day, bit by bit.

As you do, keep a running dialogue with God. Comment on each part of your day. Be glad and thankful, sorry and rueful, puzzled and satisfied, as each part suggests.

Pray as your heart wants to pray. Then give God time to respond to you.

End by enjoying God's company. (If you have a porch, or if a park bench is available, you might want to sit for a while.)

107

SUNSETS

When they have the time, people sometimes go out to watch the sunset. Even when many people are in a certain place to watch the sunset, the mood is generally subdued and reflective. A sunset belongs to everybody. No one tries to own it, although people may try to claim a place for a better view.

Sunsets evoke a natural contemplation. People "get lost" in sunsets.

When you watch a sunset, why not let it lead you into prayer? You might reflect on how everyone can enjoy the sunset just by being there and attending to it. There is no cost; there is no need for money or talent or even luck.

Everyone can enjoy God just by attending to God's presence. There is no cost, no need for talent or luck. With God, you don't even have to go outside or wait for the right time of day.

Pause before God, as you do with sunsets, just to enjoy the glory and peace of the moment.

108

WHISPER

Read a psalm or another passage of Scripture. When something strikes you, pause and reflect on it. Perhaps talk with God about it. Respond as you are moved.

Then take another moment to remember how a word, phrase, or symbol moved you.
Hold your open hands, palm up, toward you.
Bring your hands to your mouth.
Whisper the word, the phrase, the symbol into your open hands.
Close your hands in the symbolic gesture of prayer.

Let your prayer course through your body during the day. Be conscious of it when you can. Come back to it at odd moments during the day—when you're unlocking a car door, waiting for a bus, putting away groceries, waiting for the microwave to beep. You will discover a lot of situations that allow you to stop and remember your prayer.

This is a fine way "to pray always" (Luke 18:1).

109

IT ALWAYS HAPPENS

Every time you pray, two things happen:
The Spirit of God and your spirit unite.
The bond of love between you deepens.

Think about that! *Every* time you pray, the Spirit of God (all-holy, all-good, love itself) and your spirit join, and the love between you deepens!

What does that do for you? It gives you a very healthy spiritual life.

With that love conscious and active in you, you have a finer sense of what is right and wrong, what is the good and loving thing to do, and how to live out love of God and love of neighbor. What's more, that love gives you a taste for what is of God. Once you have that taste, no other will do.

110

NO WORDS

At times our hearts are so full that words are at best useless and at worst untruthful. What is true for you right now might well be beyond words, too deep for words.

Why scamper and scrape around the bottom of your soul trying to find some words? Right now they are too puny. God doesn't need our words to understand us.

Yet what you are feeling might cry out for vocal expression. If so, you can

~ groan. Most of us don't groan enough. Moaning can be good too. Develop a repertoire of moaning and groaning. (Best done in private, of course. Alone in the car with the windows rolled up. On a tractor in the middle of a field. In an ice-fishing shack. You know.)

~ cry. Weep. Wail. Whine. (Same places as suggested above. If you don't have access to any of them, cry the loudest while you vacuum the carpet or flush the toilet or use a power tool.)

~ sing sounds (joyful, noisy, enraged, despairing, contented, irritable, embarrassed, terrified, glad sounds).

Then maybe you can say, "Did you hear *that*, Lord? Now what?"

And be sure to listen to God's noises!

III

BE STILL

It is a good thing to be still.

Often it is a difficult thing to be still—even in prayer.

Praying a verse from a psalm helps to keep you aware of God's presence.

Perhaps you could try this verse.
"Be still, and know that I am God!" (Psalm 46:10).
Be still, and know that I am . . .
Be still, and know . . .
Be still . . .
Be . . .

You might find that as often as you do this, and the longer you do this, what happens is never quite the same.

PRAYER FOR GROWTH

112

JUNK FOOD

Junk-food meals? Junk-food snacks?

People are becoming increasingly conscious of diets and healthy food, and supermarkets and restaurants cater to this heightened awareness. Fat-free or sugar-free food is advertised. Milk is not just milk but is labeled skim, butter, 2 percent, vitamin D, or half-and-half (at least, it isn't really cream). Fast-food stores add salads to their menus. We make conscious choices about what we put into our bodies.

What about what goes into the soul (spirit, heart, the *you* of you)? Is it junk food or a healthy diet? How selective are you about your soul's diet? How do you feed your soul? As regularly or as carefully as you feed your body?

Take a moment and look at your soul's diet. Do you give your heart time for the comfort of friendship? your spirit time for what feeds it—music, nature, love? Do you, every day, bring your spirit to the Spirit of love, to be loved?

This is one simple way to pray:

Let yourself be conscious of being in God's presence. Let yourself know (down deep, for sure) that God is with you always, loving you always. Sink into that knowledge and enjoy God's loving you. (Your spirit will thrive!)

113

INTIMACY

This word—*intimacy*—comes from two Latin words meaning "no fear."

Think about the person or people with whom, over the course of your life, you've had a good and satisfying relationship. When you know each other, when there is friendship and love between you, intimacy is formed. And as the love and trust deepen, so does the intimacy.

No one, absolutely no one, can know you as your God knows you. No one, absolutely no one, can offer you the quality and depth of friendship that God offers you. Jesus made that so clear!

Take some time (remembering that God is with you, knowing and loving you) to examine how seriously you take God's offer of intimacy. Talk to God as your heart desires.

Later, notice how this intimacy affects your praying, "Thy will be done."

114

POCKETS

Often you don't have a lot of spare time.

At some point during the day (or evening, if you can) make yourself a pocket of time. During that pocket of time, remember that God is with you, and in God's presence look at what is going on in your life.

Pick one thing and ask God:
~ What am I supposed to be learning from this?
~ What is in it that I don't want to know?
~ How do you, my God, want me to come through this?

Be sure to give your heart time to hear your God's answer.

You might need another pocket or two.

115

PLANTING

If you are careful, how might you prepare to plant?

You know what the plant needs by way of soil and sunlight and water. You know *this* soil, *this* sunlight. You know the season for planting this plant. You know what is likely to happen.

Conscious of your God's presence with you as you plant, think about how God cares for you.

In hard times, think about bulbs. You plant bulbs before the frost. To bloom they must first freeze, die. Then, in spring, your garden is beautiful.

Let your mind and heart roam about your life.

Be grateful to your gardener God, who plants and cares for you.

Perhaps be in awe of your God's gardening all of creation!

116

PINCHING AND PRUNING

Pinching, pruning, cutting back. Any gardener knows how important these things are if a plant is to bear good fruit.

Maybe, at the time, it "hurts" the plant. But look what happens!

While pinching, pruning, cutting back your plants, think about your life. What in it needs to be pruned (even good things)?

In your God's presence, look at your life.

~ What good things clutter it, dissipate it, so there is not strength left to produce choice fruit?
~ What once-good things now are dead, but you still hold on to them?
~ What, if pinched, pruned, cut back, would result in your having life, and life in more abundance?

Spend some time talking with your God about the pain of pruning, about the life worth living.

Ask for what you need.

117

YOUR BIRTHDAY

It's your birthday!

How do you pray? Often you might think about who you are and what you want to be. That's good.

On your birthday, take time to remember God's presence. Remember that God is with you, here and now.

On your birthday, forget, for a bit, who and what you are.

Conscious that your God is with you, think about that great and good reality:
~ you are;
~ you exist;
~ you couldn't be, unless God loved you into being, and kept you there.

In God's infinite wisdom and love, God wants you to be.

Enjoy a happy birthday from your God. It is so.

118

WATERING

When watering your plants or garden, think about what you are doing.

What does water do for your plants? They cannot live, nor will they grow, without it. They will not bloom or bear fruit without it.

Then think a little more. In John's Gospel especially, Jesus promises us "living water." That living water is the Holy Spirit, the love with whom God loves God's own self. It is the love that can unite us (in "the unity of the Spirit" [Ephesians 4:3]). This love enables us to keep the great commandments—to love God and our neighbor.

Do what Jesus invites you to do: Ask for living water! Think about what this might mean for you. Let your heart respond to God's gift of living water.

119

GRADUAL INFIRMITY

As you age you might notice things:

~ You get tired faster.
~ You forget.
~ You lose (misplace) things, like keys.
~ Some body parts demand attention.
~ Even with attention, some body parts don't work right.
~ The doctor says, "The best we can do is alleviate the pain (somewhat)."
~ People spontaneously offer to help (do you look that old and in need?).

Lord, you might ask, *what do I do with this? I'm not ready for this!*

In God's presence, be aware of the changes you notice. Be aware also of how you react. Surprised? Irritated with yourself? Hoping it will get better? Talk to God about your condition.

Rest a bit in knowing that God loves you *just as you are*. Ask God to help you accept yourself *just as you are*.

Not only that, but God enjoys you, God's own creation. Whatever stage of life or growth (or deterioration!) you are in, God enjoys you in that stage. If God is satisfied, what about you? Are your standards higher than God's? Did God make a mistake in you? Hardly!

Pray that you might graciously accept your gradual infirmity—and even, possibly, enjoy the surprises of adjustment.

120

LET GO

"Let go," they say.
"Let go, let God."

Much easier said than done!
You may *really* want to let go.
But, you ask, how? And how long will it take?
Why is it so hard?
What things in your life get in the way?

"Letting go" can be an adventure with God.

Ask for self-revelation, self-understanding.
Ask for the courage and determination to make your life better.

And while you're at it,
ask God for God's self-revelation to you.
Ask God for some understanding of God's love for you.
Ask for some understanding of God's providence.

It's all part of working out your salvation.
It's all part of being whole, of being healthy and holy.

121

THE BEST WAY

What is the best way to pray?

Look in the Epistles. The Holy Spirit prays in us. The Holy Spirit prays for us when we don't know how. The power of the Holy Spirit is given to help us pray well.

Do not resist the Holy Spirit, who is in you. Do not pull back or close your ears. (It's dangerous to flirt with God like this. God understands, but there's always a chance that you'll catch that dreadful thing called hardness of heart.)

Look in the Gospels. Pay attention to what Jesus taught us about love of God and love of neighbor. Examine your ordinary, everyday life.

If how you are praying helps you live the love of God and love of neighbor, you are praying well.

Warning: This "praying well" is not static. God is always calling you to deeper intimacy.

122

EMBARRASSED!
HUMILIATED!
MORTIFIED!

The worst of it is that this time there is no one to blame but yourself.

Come to God now, in whatever way you can. In your anger or your shame, simply be in God's presence. Let God's unwavering, unconditional love wash over you, wash through you.

Let yourself know that you *are* God's loved child.

Later, with confidence, you and your God can plan how you will move through the next days. Maybe knowing that you are loved—by one no less than GOD—will help in unexpected ways.

Find out for yourself how true this is.

123

CHECK

Wood, if not dried carefully, develops a flaw called a check. Woodworkers know that the presence of a check affects the success of their proposed work. They study the wood before beginning to work. If they find a check, they study the wood even more carefully to be able to bring out the beauty inherent in it.

Every one of us is checked in some way.

With God by your side, look at the person whose "check" is proving troublesome. As a woodworker studies the checked wood, you and God study this checked person. How can you work around, or incorporate, the check in making a work of art (a good relationship)?

It might take more than one session! If the relationship is worth it to you, give it all the time it needs.

And, while spending so much time with God over the other person's "check," notice what God might be doing with yours!

124

QUESTIONS

You have faith. You believe in God. You believe God.

At times, though, you may wonder.

Questions come, questions you cannot seem to answer in any way that satisfies you. Questions about God. Questions about the Church. Questions about what you hear that the Church teaches. Questions that come up when you look seriously at your life and at what others tell you about God and what God wants. Questions that perhaps you haven't thought about, but your kids or colleagues do. And once they bring up such questions, you wonder too.

Maybe you want at least to believe, if not understand. Maybe things are so difficult that you don't care anymore what you believe or what the Church teaches.

Can you pray when you are like this?

Yes.

Pray the prayer of the child's father if you wish: *I believe; help my unbelief!* (Mark 9:24). Pray it for days, weeks, months, maybe even years. Pray it as long as it takes. It is a good prayer.

It's amazing—the slow, sure, deep growth of faith in us.

125

SOURCE

The great commandments are to love the Lord our God with all we are and all we have, and to love our neighbor as ourselves.

You must have heard that *God is love.* How do you use this knowledge to help you live?

When attempting to keep the great commandment of love, when finding it quite difficult (or altogether beyond you with respect to certain people), how do you use your knowledge that *God is love?*

Go deep into your heart, to that place where you and God meet. Gaze upon God with your mind, your heart, your whole being. (Gaze in the way you look upon a loved baby.) Immerse yourself in knowing that *God is love* (see 1 John 4:8, 16). Do this long enough and often enough that you accept the love God always offers. More and more, God's love will permeate you.

Keeping the great commandment becomes increasingly as normal as breathing.

126

FAULT

If you examine your days, day by day, there are bound to be faulty actions or omissions. You could say, "There is only one God. There are no job openings." Being faulty is quite human.

If you pick one fault that bothers you (or bothers someone you care for) and decide to do better, you might find out how hard it is. You might find that you try and try and sometimes succeed, but every so often that fault pops up most unexpectedly.

Please don't settle for "Well, that's the way I am" and give up. Stay aware of your faults and how they affect other people. Continue to try to do better.

Your prayer might be for God's mercy. For God's understanding of how you do try and still fail so often.

The Bible is full of God's mercy and compassion. You can trust it.

127

SIN

When you think about your sin, you might want to review the situation with God in something of this fashion.

I am a good person. I am.
Then, maybe, I make my sin
so small that I trivialize it
or so general that it loses meaning.
(Ask your God to help you see yourself clearly.)

Either way (trivializing sin or making it unduly general)
sets a person apart from God
with an ever-hardening heart.
(Do you suffer from hardening of the heart?
Check it out with your God.)

I *am* a good person.
Yes, you are.
But you shall be even better
as you ask your God for help
and allow yourself to receive it.
Will you? Perhaps now?

128

MUTUAL

Good relationships (marriage, friendship) are mutual. As a matter of fact, they are made by mutual self-revelation. You reveal yourself to another person, and that person reveals himself or herself to you.

This revelation is necessary for good relationships. How it happens is as different as you and the other people involved. You reveal yourself through talk, body language, and behavior.

With God, prayer is mutual self-revelation. You let God know what is happening in your life, what you are thinking and feeling, how you *are* in the various levels of your being. When you go with God to those places you don't show others and perhaps don't look at often, you are revealing yourself as totally as possible.

God is always revealing God's own self. Just listen. This kind of mutuality takes time and discipline. You might decide to start now, emptying your mind of everything and simply listening for God.

129

PREPARATION

Some people suggest that we should be open to God's grace as the fields are open to the sun and rain. Actually, there is much more involved if a crop is to grow.

First a farmer plows a field—breaks up its surface. Some farmers chisel-plow to prevent erosion and collect water. Harrowing and disking follow to break up the clumps and smooth them over. After planting, the field is ready for the sun and the rain to make the crops mature.

Imagine the farmer's work, if you would. Look at its parallel in your own life. How are you "broken up"? What is "planted" in you? How are you made ready for the sun and the rain to help you mature?

As those things happen to you, let your prayer reflect them. Let God see you broken up. As something in your life is being broken, ask God to help you prevent your erosion and collect living water in your "furrows."

What does the struggle plant in you? How do you receive the rain of God's living water and the sun of God's love?

Go to your God as you are. It will be well.

130

OBEDIENCE

When you hear the word *obedience*, do you think of children? of a school for dogs? of the law? of yourself?

Obedience is a fundamental of created existence. Take an easy example first. Ordinarily people read the manufacturer's directions or manual before dealing with a new product. Ordinarily things work better if directions are followed. But because the directions are given by human beings, another human being (you?) might figure out a better way.

God, on the other hand, does not merely make; God creates. No one will find better directions. Part of the wonder of it is that God doesn't say, "Finished!" When God creates human beings, the creation goes on and on during our pilgrimage back to God.

This ongoing creation is called providence. God provides. God leaves you free to be obedient to God's plan. You can be disobedient. But you cannot make poor choices without harm to yourself and others. (Jesus' obedience to his Father redeemed all of us!)

Because of your creaturely limitations, good choices are not always clear or easy to make. So you are invited to plead with God, repeatedly, for assistance. Trust in the answer he gave Paul: "My grace is sufficient for you" (2 Corinthians 12:9).

Obedience to God's plan, God's will for you, has the inevitable result of your having life, and life in abundance.

131

WORKS OF ART

People go to museums. Much time is spent looking at, studying, and enjoying beautiful things. Other people might be present or not.

People go to concerts. Much time is spent listening to and enjoying beautiful music. Part of the enjoyment is that the music is live and they are part of an audience.

How much more fully alive are you when you move from observer (no matter how knowledgeable) or listener (no matter how discriminating) to artist!

When you engage in making the work of art, when you put your talent, your person, into the object or the music, you do not merely enjoy the work of art; you make it! That is a whole other experience, with a whole other range of enjoyment.

In the epistle to the Ephesians (2:10, JB) you are called "God's work of art." You are God's work of art.

The wonder of God's creativity is that God does not make you a painting, a statue, a building, a musical score—a finished product. God wants you to have a part in becoming the final work of art you are destined to be.

Today, with God at your side, take a good look at your inmost being. What do you look like? What do you sound like? For what are you, God's work of art, thankful?

How does your heart want to be with your God?

132

IS IT GOD'S WILL?

Is it God's will?

You probably cannot be sure.

Of this much you can be sure: If as a matter of course you want to do God's will and you lead a good, moral life, then knowing God's will is not always that difficult. If you make a mistake, you can quickly remedy it.

Think. If you crack open an egg and your nose is filled with the smell of sulfur, what do you know right away? Well, that the egg is bad. Inedible. If you eat it, you will become ill.

If what you are thinking about doing "smells bad," it is not God's will. If you do it anyway, you will get sick. Sin.

So much is that simple.

PRAYER THAT ASKS AND TRUSTS

133

STRENGTH

You never really know what the day will bring.

Oh, you may have a calendar and know which things are planned. But what about the unexpected? the surprises? What about the inconveniences, especially those precipitated by people you find unpleasant? What about those times when more is being asked of you—and your time is already spoken for and your financial resources are strained?

As the day starts—and as it goes on—ask God's help to remember that the living, loving presence of God is with you. Ask your God for the honesty, the strength, and the kindness (and whatever else you especially need) to deal well with the incidents of the day.

Tell God you do believe (or ask God to make you willing to believe) what the epistle says: "We know that all things work together for good for those who love God" (Romans 8:28).

Ask God to make you, your words, and your actions good during this day. Trust that all things will work unto good.

Take another moment to let yourself sink into *who* God is. Worship, as your faith leads you.

134

ALL I HAVE, BOTH SIDES

In the parable of the prodigal son, Jesus tells you that the Father says to you, "All that is mine is yours" (Luke 15:31).

Jesus reveals to you the infinite generosity of your God.

Now it's your turn. Let your mind go over "all you have": all you are and all that you hope for. Spend a little time on this.

Then hear again Jesus telling you what the Father says to you: "All that is mine is yours." Let your mind and heart, your whole self, nibble at what that might mean.

With what generosity can you pray to the Father, "All that is mine is yours"? Can you, wholeheartedly, mean it? If you can, pray this way.

If you are not up to it, tell God you are not up to it. God knows, and he knows why better than you do.

If you can, ask God to enable you to pray with this attitude.

If you don't want to do that either, let God know.

Ask God for what you need.

Gladly live with what God gives you.

135

ASK

Be aware that God is with you.
Know that you are in the presence of God.

In God's presence, then,
think about how things are with you,
what it is that you need or want,
the people who concern you,
what you might do about these various concerns.

Then ask God to give you whatever it is that God wants to give you.

You might want to take some time to think about this: Why would you be glad and satisfied to ask for what God wants to give you?

136

GUARDIAN ANGELS

For a long time Christians have believed in guardian angels.

Angels are God's special messengers to people. These pure spirits love and praise and adore God. They help us come to God, God's way.

Tradition says that each person has a guardian angel (as do nations and other groups). It is a good thing to pray to your angel. Angels know God better and more intimately than you do. They understand more. With their love of God and of you, you have strong advocates.

Ask your angel to protect you and your loved ones. Ask your angel to help you make wise decisions. Ask your angel to pray with you as you worship your God.

How might praying with an angel help? People sometimes say they cannot sing a solo, but they sing well enough in a group, surrounded by other singers. It just might be that you pray better when praying in the company of stronger pray-ers. Angels are very strong pray-ers!

137

OTHER EYES

What is the first thing you think of when you open your eyes in the morning? (Wondering where the night went?) What is the next thing you think about?

Even if it means setting the alarm ten minutes or so ahead (groan and sigh if you want), are you willing to try this?

When you first open your eyes (well, after the alarm has been stilled), thank God for bringing you back from sleep. Thank God for bringing you and your family safely through the night.

Maybe you want to continue your "Good morning, God!" routine in bed (so no one will know you're awake). Or you can stand, kneel, sit, or walk as you continue your morning greeting to your God.

For what do you want to ask God as this new day begins? Set yourself up with your God to live this day fully and well. Allow the Holy Spirit to be effective in you.

Remember that Jesus said, "I have come to bring life and life in abundance" (see John 10:10). Ask for abundance. Be willing to do what you have to do, sacrifice what you have to sacrifice, to have the abundance God wills for you. Ask God for the grace to see the people and events of the day with other eyes, with the eyes of faith. Ask God to help you be open to God's gifts to you, God's way, this day.

And be glad for the rest of your life.

138

WANTING

It's easy to remember to pray when you want something. Sometimes that's true of phone calls, isn't it? Some people remember to call only when they want something.

That's not a bad thing. In fact, the act of asking is also often an act of hope. You ask the person who you think is able to grant the favor, and you hope he or she will do it.

Suppose, in this prayer time, you remember you are in God's presence. (That is always true.) Suppose, in your God's presence, you make a list of everything you want. Have concern neither for time nor for money. Set no limits. If you want it, put it on the list.

When you are finished (you might take several days if you want), you and God look at it together.

What does the list tell you about yourself? In a very real way your desires define the kind of person you are.

Look, with your God, at your list of desires, at what those desires say about you.

Sort the list by asking yourself, *Which of these things would I be worrying about if I were on my deathbed?*

Then ask God to help you with what you need most.

139

ASKING

Following Jesus' example, you are invited to pray in all the circumstances of your life, in all your relationships, about all that concerns you. That's a given.

Another given is this: "Not my will but yours be done" (Luke 22:42).

Probably you know this, and maybe you mutter it through gritted teeth. What you ask seems so right, so sensible, so necessary; how could God be God and not grant it?

One of the ways to pray yourself through this with trustful satisfaction is to let your prayer become contemplative.

Pray with all the desire of your heart. When that is said and done, let yourself sink into God. You may be filled with anxiety, anguish, or longing. You may be as happy as can be or bored silly. However you are, just sink into God. Let God take the lead with you.

God is not likely to change external circumstances. But this kind of prayer does make you open to hearing God speak to your heart.

Then, no matter what you asked or how it was or was not granted, all will be well. For indeed, you are loved!

140

YOUR CHOICE

Often you may be told to "trust God."

Have you ever thought about how much God trusts you?

It's called God's gift of freedom. You are free to choose how you act and what kind of person you make of yourself with what you have. You are free to accept God in your life or not.

Look at how God trusts you. God—at all times and in all places—offers you God's own loving and unfailing friendship. God *never* turns against you or leaves you.

Your own experience must tell you that a good friendship is a two-way street. Both friends give; both receive. Friendship with God is something like that. God gives more; God makes it possible for you to *be*. God makes you good. Then God offers you friendship.

Just think: God trusts you, leaves you free to pursue the friendship or not.

Why not spend this prayer time with God on the issue of mutual trust and what it means to you? After that, you might bring up the subject of the state of your friendship and what it is you deeply long for.

141

LONGING

Suppose that you wanted something badly, you received it, and still . . . it wasn't enough. You longed for more.

Most people experience longing. Things are not enough; relationships are not enough. We always want more of whatever we have.

Karl Rahner, one of the best theologians of this century, called prayer "a longing." Longing shows us that we are made by God and for God, that nothing and no one else *totally* satisfies us in every way or for long.

Let yourself experience longing. Take your time. Wallow in it a bit if you wish. Then, as a sunflower naturally turns to the sun, let your heart turn to your God. For light. For fullness. Turn to God, asking God to help you live in such a way that, when you die, all your great longings will be filled.

If your longing is too much for words (and it might well be), just be with God with these concerns on your mind.

142

SANTA CLAUS

God, most certainly, is not Santa Claus. Yet for the moment, pretend you are a child again and make a list of all your desires. Everything you want, need, hope for. Make it as long, good, mischievous, shameful as you want. No one will see it but you and your God.

Hold your list in your heart. Look at it with your God.

As you do this together, you realize how this list of what you want, need, and hope for defines you as the person you are.

Be with God as the person you are.

Tell God what you want, knowing all the time that God knows, God understands, God loves you unconditionally, and you are utterly safe.

Be with God just as you are.

Let God be with you, as God is.

Let yourself be healed by God's love.

143

EQUIPMENT

Just think about
E-mail, fax, Internet, phone, radio, copier
and all the other sorts of equipment
we use for communication—
all requiring some skill
some equipment
and some money.
Not so
for the most important
communication in our life!
No technology is needed
to plug into
God
save that which was issued us
at birth:
mind and heart!
Take a moment to be grateful.
Take a moment to be thankful.

Remember, you always have yourself. Your God is always with you.

144

TAKE A CHANCE!

What about taking a chance with God? You know your situation, your need, your desire. You ask God to grant what you want or need.

So far so good.

Now go further, if you will.
Take a chance.
Although you ask strongly for what you want,
let there be another layer of reality.
Perhaps you might say,
"This I ask, unless, God,
in your great wisdom and love,
you see that this is not good for me
or for those around me.
In which case,
in your great wisdom and love,
please give me something better!"

Jesus asked for his passion and death not to happen. They did. God raised Jesus from the dead—glorious and immortal. How can you beat that?

145

WATCH ME!

"Watch me!"

As children learn to do things by themselves, don't they ask you (incessantly), "Watch me!"? Then they proudly proceed to show you what they can do. If they fail, they try it again, with the cry, "Watch me this time!" If they fail badly, aren't you there to comfort, help, and encourage?

Do you think you can love your children more than God loves you? Your children are right to trust you. Aren't you right to trust your God to be no less comforting, helping, and encouraging?

One difference is that you do not have to say to God, "Watch me!" God does, all the time, lovingly watch you.

In the Bible's book of Wisdom it says, "God is witness of their inmost feelings, and a true observer of their hearts, and a hearer of their tongues" (1:6).

Why not take advantage of God as your children do of you?

Why not say to God, "Watch me!" and mean it?

If you have something to say about this to God, say it now.

And be glad!

146

FAITH (OR LACK OF IT)

This is not easy.

There are times when your spirit feels empty. There seems to be nothing to support or nourish it. You might wonder if God really exists or if he cares about you. You just do not feel anything. Past experiences, whatever they are, don't seem to count. Nothing has any meaning. Were you duped into believing in God?

Faith and hope are difficult virtues. In a way you don't care; in a way you do. Life is just barren. Is it worth it?

What do you do in a time like this? You don't want to lie in your prayer, telling God things you don't believe. What can you honestly say?

Now might be a time to repeat often the prayer of the man in the Gospel: "I do have faith. Help the little faith I have!" (Mark 9:24, JB).

That might be your prayer for a long time. Be faithful. Spring follows winter.

147

BEYOND UNDER-STANDING

Society and our education often lead us to think that just about anything can be made better, can be fixed, and can be understood.

Realistically that is just not so.

Things made of parts wear out and fall apart. Some physical pain might be alleviated but not cured. As for understanding—at times the most important things are not understood. They are experienced or they are known; they are not understood.

So why should it surprise us that the deepest things of God are not understood?

When we have faith in God, we know in a way that is beyond understanding. When we have peace in adverse circumstances, we experience it beyond understanding. When we meet God in our innermost self, there is an encounter, but it is beyond understanding. We don't have to understand in order for the experience to be real.

Go to that deep-down place in your heart and meet your God. If you are willing, tell God you don't understand how God can be so good, how God can love you unconditionally, all of the time.

Ask God to help you *believe* it. Ask God to help you *live* it, making your faith in that unconditional love affect your day-by-day living.

Then rest in God's presence for a while.

PRAYER THAT HEALS

148

ROCK REMINDERS

Pick up a rock small enough to fit in one hand. See if you can find one that is dense and heavy for its size.

Pray this prayer when you are feeling dense and heavy with guilt from the memory of things you regret having done. Reflect on something that causes you suffering, anxiety, or some heaviness due to a grudge or a desire for vengeance. Reflect on whatever else burns you up and burdens you. Let the rock symbolize this weight that you're carrying.

~ Hold the rock in both hands, feeling its weight.
~ Concentrate on the dense, dark, burdensome feelings in you.
~ One by one let them flow from you into the rock.
~ When you are finished, ask God to let the other burdensome feelings you might not remember flow out of you into the rock.
~ Feel, with God's grace, the rock getting heavier.

In your prayer ask God's forgiveness for your part in the situation. Ask for healing and liberation. As a symbol of God's mercy and your willingness to be freed from these burdens, dispose of the rock. If you are near water, toss it into the deepest part. Or bury it as deeply as you can. Think of some way to put it away from you.

Ask your God to give you the grace to live more freely and strongly as you are relieved of these burdens.

Having received God's mercy, how will you be more merciful to others?

149

FORGIVING

Certain things are relatively easy to forgive. There are those, however, that might make you cry out, "I'll never forgive *that!*" Your (almost) whole being means it.

After a while (deep wounds take longer to heal than superficial ones) you might need to go back to Jesus on the cross. He prayed, "Father, forgive them; for they do not know what they are doing" (Luke 23:34). Probably Pilate, the chief priests and leaders, and the Roman soldiers thought they knew what they were doing. To a point they did. But in reality? (Do you think Pilate knew he'd be mentioned in the Christian creed for over two thousand years?)

Be, in your mind and heart, with Jesus, who is dying on the cross. Hear his prayer. See him look at you, into your heart.

Your heart is bruised, maybe broken. Jesus surely knows what that is like. Be together in the pain you both know.

Jesus trusted that his beloved Father would work all things unto good (see Romans 8:28). Ask Jesus to help you have that trust in your pain too. Take as long as you need. After you've prayed as honestly as you can, for as long as you need (days? weeks? months? years?), surrender yourself to God's truly tender mercy. Leave also to God's tender mercy the people who have hurt you.

There really is nothing else to do.

150

FAILURE

When you fail—at work, at home, in a relationship, in yourself—when you are wrong or confused or just not up to it, how do you go to your God in prayer? Miserable? Blaming? Bruised? Broken? Despairing? How?

Go as you are. (It's futile to try to fake it with God!)
God knows—the why and what,
the how and where of it all.
God also knows the YOU under the failure.

You are safe with your God.
God will never turn away from you.
Nor is God likely to save you
from the consequences of your actions,
but God will see you through it all—
if you allow yourself to know God's loving presence,
if you allow yourself to receive God's enlivening love.

Will you?

151

DOCTORS

Doctor, dentist, therapist. Each is (we hope) a skilled professional. Each is (surely) a human being.

When you or someone you are concerned about needs to visit a health-care professional, pray.

~ Pray for the doctor, that he or she may have insight and skill.
~ Pray for the patient, that diagnoses may be correct and treatment effective.
~ Pray for doctor and patient, that they use the gifts God gave them.
~ Pray for all concerned, that they learn well from their meeting.

Of course, this can be prayed in your own words. This can be prayed in your mind and heart, in your God's presence.

152

HATE

At times you are so disturbed by what someone did (or didn't do), you hate that person. You can hardly help yourself. You hate. Fiercely.

Then it strikes you.

You are *not* a hateful person. Perhaps you pride yourself on being a loving person, a peaceful person. Or at least a normally good person. But certainly not a hating one. And here you are.

Remember that hate is not the opposite of love. *Indifference* (not caring) is contrary to love. When you hate, you are *not* indifferent.

Hate can overtake you when the offense was dreadful. It is normal to experience hate under such circumstances. But it is not normal to feed the hate, to wallow in it. That will rot your soul. Nobody is worth that cost!

In your imagination go to Jesus. He had cause to hate some of the people around him. Talk with him about how he handled it. Go beyond talking in this prayer. Be close to Jesus. Let his love, his strength, his whatever it took not to hate, flow into you.

Ask him to free you from this hatred. (Try to mean it. If it's too hard, tell him that also.)

Do this as often as you need to.

153

HAVE A PHYSICAL

Health-care professionals tell us to get a physical every so often. Some of us do; some of us don't. Some people don't see the need for it, and others can't afford it or are too busy.

What if someone asked you, "When was your last spiritual?" When was the last time you checked your soul's health? your love level of God and neighbor? the functioning of your soul's hearing and seeing? your soul's vital signs?

Before you go to the doctor, you might think about the pain or dysfunction that your body suffers. You might think about how to describe it. You're probably ready to name the medications you already take.

Before you go to someone you can trust with your "spiritual," take some time with God to examine the pain or dysfunction your *spirit* suffers. You might think about how to describe it. Maybe you are ready to name what you are doing to improve your relationship with God and neighbor.

This is time well spent. You can do it anytime, in a place of your choosing. You don't need an HMO or any plan or any money at all. Just do it, and let your heart pray as its desire leads you.

154

IT'S CATCHING!

Like it or not, how you are, what you do,
affects others—
just as how they are,
what they do, affects you.
It's catching!
When someone (especially someone you love and trust)
offends you, hurts you,
does you wrong in a serious way,
how do you forgive him or her?

In your prayer, hold that person before God.
You might say of a loved, trusted person
who has badly injured you:
God, that one acted out of character!
(Why? Who knows?)
Ask your God to help you be willing
to give that person back to him- or herself,
to help that person ease back
into the character that is normal.
Ask God to help you restore that person to value.

Wait. Listen. God answers in surprising ways when
God so wills.

155

OSMOSIS

Think of a place you especially like to be. Imagine yourself being there under the best of conditions. Enjoy being there.

Jesus comes and greets you. Hear Jesus saying your name. Sit together (or take a walk or do whatever you like).

Let Jesus know how, down deep, you are: angry, worried, glad, resentful, tired, frustrated, satisfied, whatever your combination of things might be.

If finding the right words is a burden, invite Jesus to know your mind, and know your heart, with you. Then lean into Jesus (maybe he puts his arm around you). Let some of his wisdom, strength, courage, compassion, love (whatever it is that you need this day) flow into you. It will.

Do this as often as you like. All will be well.

156

YOUR HEART

The word heart *refers to spirit, soul, the inmost part of you, what most deeply and definitively makes you* you.

No matter what is going on in your life this day—worry, fear, anger, shame, guilt, exhaustion, confusion, resentment, boredom—become as quiet, as still as you can. Go to that place inside of you where you and God meet. Be in God's presence.

Without words, without explanation or excuse or defense, look at your heart with God. Know, with God, how it is and what is in it. Take your time. Wordlessly hold your heart before your God. Your need, your desire, your yearning *is* known. Take your time.

God so much wants your healing, your wholeness, that Jesus was sent for you. Trust in God's concern for you.

End your conscious time with God in whatever way your heart wants to pray.

157

NOT ENOUGH

You read articles or listen to talk shows about your self-image, your self-esteem. What they say, generally, is right—but it doesn't go far enough.

People give you advice. Often it isn't bad advice—but it doesn't go far enough.

You think about what *you'd* like to do—but perhaps your understanding isn't deep enough or your decision isn't wise enough.

Much of life is just plain *not enough*. It may serve your purpose to a degree; it may be effective on a certain level; it may have the spoken approval of friends and family—but it is not enough.

That is why it is so important to "sink into God" as a vital part of your prayer. Be quietly attentive to God.

When you have come to "It *is* enough," then you and God can be together most peacefully.

158

ILLNESS OR AGING

When you become ill or old or when you are facing a serious medical procedure, you are welcome to receive the Sacrament of the Sick. You can come to the church community for this amazing healing sacrament.

In the presence of all the angels and saints and the people with you, ask your God for healing. (Healing means that the deepest, fullest, complete *you* is healed of all that is not holy—whether or not you are cured of your physical illness.) You are helped to be at peace, ready to greet your God in whatever way God wants. The sacrament may help with a physical cure, or it may not. But as you enter into it, it does making healing yours.

Speak to people who have received this sacrament. Ask them, if they are willing to tell you, what difference this sacrament makes to them. Don't be surprised if they talk with you about a peace, a contentment, a rare joy that fills them. How things fall into place, how all that is important is well. Look at their faces, their body language. Something very good has happened.

Words cannot explain it. They are filled with a rare happiness. Faith and hope and love are unmistakable. It is holy. It is sacred. It is totally right.

In your physical suffering (age counts), pray the prayers of the Sacrament of the Sick. That magnificent treasure is yours for the asking.

159

WHEN YOU DIE

When it is time for you to die, how do you want to be with God?

In the last days or hours of your being alive on this earth, how do you want to address your God?

People who are very ill say that sometimes they are in too much pain to pray; sometimes they are too drugged to be able to pray.

Suppose you give it some time now.

Really think about it. How do you want your God to find you as you leave this earthly life? What might you want to be saying to God? In what "order" do you want your mind and heart, your spirit to be? Remember, it will be the last thing you say to God before meeting face-to-face.

Give it some prayer time. You can delete, erase, change what you think as often as you wish. When you find what suits you, pray that way. Every day.

When the time comes for you to die, that prayer will pray itself. The Spirit in you will only make it stronger.

May your death be an eager and peaceful one!

PRAYER THAT PAYS ATTENTION

160

PREVENTION

Why should you pray?

There are as many reasons as there are people and circumstances. But here is one reason that is always appropriate for every person: prevention!

Suppose you are healthy. What do you do to remain healthy? to strengthen your body to make it strong and therefore prevent illness? Think of what you do for your body: eat, sleep, bathe, work, play, exercise, take vitamins or food supplements, do what your doctor says about this or that. Most of it you probably do as a matter of course. You use preventive measures against illness.

How do you take care of your soul? How do you keep your soul healthy and help it be immune to evil? Think about it.

One essential measure is prayer. How you pray depends on you, but basic parts of prayer are worship, praise, thanksgiving, and supplication. One of the things you ask for daily (it's important enough to be in the Lord's Prayer) is to be "delivered from evil." You want to be preserved from doing evil (consciously or not) and to deal with—in a healthy way—the evils imposed on you.

Nothing helps like prayer truly prayed!

161

VORTEX

If you are waiting for the light to change so you can cross a busy street, look at the traffic. Watch the flow or the gridlock. Watch for the moment when one lane of traffic stops as another starts. Feel the power of the stopping and the starting and the complication of turning vehicles. Feel the power in the intersection.

Let your mind wander around the traffic of your life. Attend to the flow (or gridlock) of the people and circumstances in it. Be conscious, if you will, of the power of God in the people and events of your life—and in you. Remember the line in the epistle that says, "All things work together for good for those who love God" (Romans 8:28). That includes both flow and gridlock.

Perhaps you'll want to thank God for the traffic of your life and for the power of God's loving presence in your personal vortex. (Please don't forget to listen after you've had your say.)

162

PRESENCE

When you think about the deepest place in your heart, whose presence do you most enjoy? (Name someone to yourself and to God.)

Then, with God as your companion, think . . . muse . . . remember: What is it about this person that attracts you? that gives you life? How does this person enable you to live more fully?

Ask God to help you be conscious of this person's presence. Using that as a starting point, move into a true awareness of God's presence. (The Holy Spirit *is* God's presence.)

Get lost in the awesomeness of it, the implications of it, what it can do in your life, if you allow it.

Pray the prayer your heart urges on you.

163

TAPES

Perhaps, if you drive alone a great deal, you play audiotapes. You might receive a considerable amount of good information from them. Whether they are explicitly of a religious nature or not, they might be a good lead-in to prayer.

When the tape is complete (or stop it along the way if that suits you), take time to

- ~ be quiet;
- ~ consciously be in your God's presence;
- ~ think about what you just heard (or some part of it);
- ~ talk (think, be) with God about it: how you understand it, how it does (or doesn't) fit in with what you think;
- ~ think of what you might learn from it;
- ~ ponder how you might use it for your good and the good of other people;
- ~ be quiet again.

Pray as your heart wants to pray.

164

SAVORING

Go over your day or week or month.

What in it—people, events, thoughts, or experiences—gave you pleasure? What in it did you relish? What in it would you be tempted to smack your lips over?

It could be any one of countless things. Looking at a baby. Watching the play of sunlight on a landscape or an object. Seeing something beautiful. Hearing music that touches your soul. Getting a compliment. What is it for you?

Take that instance and savor it. Relish it. Delight in it. Enjoy it. Enjoy remembering it.

And in the savoring, thank the God who gave you this gift.

165

GLANCE

When people who know and love each other well are in a room with other people, and something is said that has meaning for them, they glance at each other. Both know that the other knows, that the other understands.

For this way of praying you only need to remember to do it.

What you really believe (as opposed to what you say or think from what you might have been taught but never really examined) is crucial.

Do you believe in God? Do you believe that God dwells in you? (Think about what Jesus said—that he and the Father would take up their abode in you.)

If you truly believe that you can meet God in that down-deep place of your heart, then looking at God is a quite simple and very good way to pray.

Knowing that God is in you, send God a loving glance every so often. You know the power of a glance. You have probably received (and given) glances that send a message: "I love you." "Don't even think of doing that!" "How could you!" "Stop it!" "Help!"

Give God a wordless, loving glance of your heart. Do it often during the day. Such a loving prayer can be far more eloquent than words.

Praying like this makes a difference in your life.

All during this day, when something is said that has meaning for you, give your God a loving glance of the heart. You know that God knows. You know that God understands. Give your God a loving glance of the heart.

Often.

166

WEDDING RINGS

Look at your wedding ring.

Think about what it means.

Think about how it relates you to your spouse, to your children, to your families.

Think about *what* you do and *how* you do it. How does it all come from your being related to these special people in your life?

When everything that you do with, to, for, or because of them honors your marriage vows, then everything you do with, to, for, or because of them is an act of love deepening your commitment.

Look at your wedding ring.

Think about your baptism.

Think about how baptism relates you to God and to all of God's people.

Think about *what* you do day by day and *how* you do it.

When what you do and how you do it honors your baptism (your relationship with God), then everything you do deepens your relationship with God.

You might want to spend some time with God, musing about your day-to-day living.

167

OUR "SHY" GOD

Whoever thought of calling God "shy"? Think about the suggestion.

When, in your prayer,
you talk and talk and talk some more,
ending with something like
"Well, that's it for now, God,"
does God outshout your monologue?
(Hardly ever.)

When, in your prayer,
you talk and talk and talk some more,
give God at least equal time
to respond to you.
(Giving God more-than-equal time
is an even better idea.)
Listen to your "shy" God.
Don't be surprised
if you hear the message at a later, unexpected time.
Don't be surprised if you hear the message
from an unexpected person.
God's ways are not our ways!

168

OH!

What brings you to exclaim, "Oh!" or "Ah!" or just catch your breath in delighted wonder? A sunrise or sunset? Fallen snow as yet unmarred? Feeling, for the first time, the baby move in your womb? A tender parent with a child? A very old person relating to a very young person? A musical passage? A wonderful fragrance? Welcomed warmth or coolness? A memory? What brings you to that breath-catching, silent moment?

When those moments come, be engrossed in them, as you usually are.

Take another moment to be conscious—with God—of the poignant beauty of the moment. Enjoy it with your God, whose love creates all that is present and whose love gives all presents their special goodness.

Let your heart praise or bless or thank God, or just enjoy the moment with the God who loves to give you such good things.

169

NOW

What, for sure, do you have?
Now.
What, for sure, can you use?
Now.
When, for sure, can you be yourself?
Now.

Now, aware of the presence of your God, reflect:
What is your attitude toward *now?*
Are your *nows* never here, but generally in the past?
in the future?
Are you grateful for the *now* that God is giving you?
Do you enjoy *now?*
Now, how do you want to live?
You and your God think about it together.
Ask God about your *now.*
Then, with God's help,
live it!

170

NOT OFTEN

Not often, but sometimes during life, there are moments.

Moments without any sense of time.

Moments when you are so involved—mind, body, heart, and soul—that you might know nothing but that you are alive here and now, in this moment.

It might be when you are with another person, sharing a special soul-knowledge of one another. It might be a moment when you are involved in music or nature.

Later, reflect on those moments.
Know the timeless joy of them.
Know God's presence in them.
Know that they are a foretaste of eternal life.

171

GOOD TASTE

In what way do you have good taste? In food? In clothes? In interior decorating? In friends?

When you think about it, how did you acquire that noted good taste? Was it in you already? Did you notice it in others? Did you acquire it through experimentation, study, or discussion?

One of the psalms says to "taste and see that the LORD is good" (Psalm 34:8). Now there's good taste! (To be able to "taste" the things of the Lord and judge the taste rightly is to have wisdom.)

Surely you have some taste of the Lord and the things of the Lord. Just as surely your taste can be refined.

Pay attention. Notice good people. Pray to know what is of God. Converse with holy people. Most of all, be good friends with the Holy Spirit, who dwells in you.

When you have this taste, no other taste will do!

172

SLOW DOWN!

You want to pray.

You cannot quiet your mind. You keep thinking of things you have to do.

Ask God's help.

Look at your day: all you are involved in, all that is expected of you, all you need to take care of.

Think of your day as if it were a car in motion. How fast is it going? 31 mph? 78 mph? 14 mph? 89 mph?

Look at the speed at which you are living.

Take control of the speed of your life. Gradually let up on the accelerator. Let up some more. Begin to raise your foot.

When your car gently rolls to a stop, spend some time with God.

173

EVERYDAY PRAYER

Much of your prayer is probably everyday prayer—concerning the people, events, laughter, frustration, humdrum of every day. That is good—good in itself, good for what it might lead to.

Many of your conversations are probably everyday conversations—concerning the common things of the day. With good friends this is so, but everyday conversation is not enough for good friends.

The same is true with God. Everyday prayer is good, but it is not enough.

"We have to talk." "I need to talk with you."

Do you say such things to your closer friends? Probably. Do you say such things to your God?

God's response invariably is, "I am with you always" (Matthew 28:20).

Make time to talk with God at length, in depth. You know that God understands you and loves you more than anyone else ever could.

And maybe, just maybe, in a quiet moment you might hear God saying to you, "We have to talk. When do you want to get together?"

What a glorious invitation—to you with your concerns—for a grand and great time with your God.

Accept the invitation.

174

LISTEN

If you read the Gospels and pray from what strikes you, you might follow this suggestion:

In John's Gospel Jesus invites us to follow him, to keep his word. Then Jesus promises that he and the Father would "make our home with [you]" (John 14:23, JB).

Probably you try to do what Jesus asks—at least most of the time.

If you do, do you believe these words of his?

And if you do, *listen.*

If the Father and the Son (whose Spirit is always loving) have taken up their abode in you, listen to them talking about the place where they live—you.

How do you respond to them?

175

EARS

They have ears but do not hear.

Most of us have selective hearing.
Not just for music
or shutting out street noise
but also for what someone else is saying.

We're too busy,
too intent on getting the job done,
not interested;
we don't think it's our business.
So what is said (and what is meant) is not heard;
even though it is important to the other person,
even though it might provide comfort.

In your prayer of reviewing the day with your God,
look at what you did.
But also look at what you did not do,
and pray as your heart needs to pray.

176

ONE OF THOSE DAYS

When you are having "one of those days," everything goes wrong. To make it worse, you drop things, forget things, get irritable, snap at people, become disgusted with yourself or angry with others.

When nothing seems to be going right, pause.

Pause and go down deep inside to that place where you and God meet. (If you have a demanding child at this moment, perhaps you can hold and comfort the child while you pause.)

Just be there, knowing you are loved just as you are. Let your God hold and comfort you, as you might a child. Bask for a few moments in the love that is always being given to you.

Things have to be dealt with. Let them fall into perspective.

Keeping mindful of God's presence, go on. The *what* of what you need to do will not change. The *how* of how you do it will.

PRAYER INTO CONTEMPLATION

A story is told of a family, from a village bordering on the Mediterranean Sea, that immigrated to the United States.

Because the family was of meager financial means, the villagers took a collection for them, a collection mostly of bread and cheese and a sausage or two.

The family sailed in steerage.

Every day they ate bread and cheese, cheese and bread, with an occasional bite of sausage.

A bit more than a week into the journey, the young son told his father that he wanted something different to eat. His father understood. Warning the boy not to tell his mother, he gave his son a small coin to purchase a treat.

Surprisingly the boy did not return. Worried (and not telling his wife), the man searched for him.

To the man's dismay he found his son in the dining room, sitting alone at a table full of food and eating heartily.

"I can't pay for this!" the father gasped.

"Father, all the food comes with the money for the passage," answered the boy as he returned the small coin to his father.

This collection of ways to pray cannot end without inviting you to the dining room.

Bread and cheese (with an occasional bite of sausage) might be adequate. But why settle for stale cheese sandwiches when your extravagantly generous God invites you daily to a feast?

The "bread and cheese" (even with an occasional bite of sausage) of this story are all the ways of praying that focus on you, me, other people, and the things and circumstances in our lives. Certainly all this prayer is as adequate and good as cheese sandwiches with sausages. But it is not yet the feast of experiencing God, of knowing God with the fuller knowledge of love.

Attending in prayer to the things of daily living is an important first step. With God's grace it can lead you into the dining room. When it does, God teaches you on the interior. God brings you to places you cannot go alone. The price of that journey? Letting God be God. Setting aside your own self (in this context, a cheese sandwich) in order to have the feast (God). It requires going to Jesus as brother and allowing him to lead you to his Father, God. It means being aware of the indwelling of the Holy Spirit in you, but focusing on God.

You cannot do it by yourself. Nor can you earn or deserve it. God gives this to you. All you can do is be willing.

A sign of willingness is asking and waiting. God does marvelous things to you! St. Thomas Aquinas says that we come from God and return to God by a movement of the heart.

Let your heart be moved. Let yourself accept God's invitation to God's feast, a feast so far beyond what you can see and hear, beyond what can be measured and counted, beyond words and ideas, that it stretches you to consider it. Please, allow yourself to be stretched. Bon appétit!

177

DEEP THINKING

Contemplate? Me?" might be your response to the suggestion. "That's for the great saints, not me!" Many people feel that way. You may be cheating yourself if you do.

Contemplate. Words fade into silence. Yet you are full. Think of how you contemplate your new wedding ring, a baby, a loved face, a beautiful scene, a treasured letter or gift. You do this wordlessly, yet knowing what it means.

Contemplate. To make a temple with. To make a holy space.

You were made holy at baptism.

You make a holy space within you when you pray, when you remind yourself that you are in God's presence, and this reminder affects how you think, speak, and act.

God invites you to this wordless intimacy. Don't worry about "doing it right." God is always with you, helping.

Just do it.

The truth is, you probably have been doing it for a long time. Recognizing it, and being conscious of what a wonderful way it is to pray, may bring even more intimacy with God to your life.

Just do it.

178

MEDITATION

Often meditation is described as thinking about something. There are a number of prescribed ways to meditate prayerfully. Use what is helpful to you.

This is one simple way to meditate. Choose a Gospel story. Read it slowly and thoughtfully two or three times. If you have privacy, read it aloud. Ask yourself these questions:

~ Who are the people in the story?
~ What are they doing?
~ What is the result?
~ What did it mean to them?
~ What can I learn from this story?
~ When I turn to God, what have I to say about it?
~ Do I remember to listen in case God has a response?

This is a good way to pray from Scripture. When you can, pick a word or a phrase from it and repeat it to yourself during the day. In this way your meditation stays alive in you. It might lead you into quiet, listening time.

Try it and see.

179

THINKING BACK

Reminiscing is frequently pleasurable. For the moment let your mind wander back to those things that, when you engage in them, absorb you completely. Things that make you lose track of time. Things that render you deaf to voices or noises around you. You do not think in words about what you are doing. There is no need or inclination to speak.

What, in your past, produced this feeling in you? What produces it now?

Reading . . . doing some art work . . . writing . . . walking on a beach or in the woods or beside railroad tracks . . . sitting on the beach or in a cornfield or on a mountain . . . hanging out . . . singing . . . letting your feet dangle in a stream . . . dancing . . . cross-stitching . . . playing a musical instrument . . . working on a car engine . . . photographing . . . painting . . . gardening . . . hiding in some secret place and being alone.

What is it that, for you, is thoroughly absorbing and enjoyable?

Go back to a way of praying that you particularly like. Let yourself become absorbed in whatever it means for you. Become as thoughtless as you are when doing something else you love doing. Be as alive, as active as you are in those other things; only this time be alive in your prayer and in the presence of God.

180

QUITE ALIVE

When are you quite alive, not thinking in words, not speaking words, but *knowing* what is pleasing you beyond conscious thought or speech?

Different things move different people, for instance,
~ holding a sleeping baby,
~ seeing a baby discover her toes,
~ watching a young child successfully doing something for the first time,
~ attending a loved one's graduation or wedding or concert,
~ looking at your own good photography or video,
~ watching a sunset, falling snow, a storm.
Let your mind wander over those things that reduce you to a silence that you love.

If you can recall a prayer or part of the liturgy, let your mind go back to your favorite words. Savor them wordlessly, thoughtlessly, as you savor a thing that brings you to a silence that you love. Stay in the silence, in your God's presence. (Remember, God's language is the language of silence.)

181

BEING KNOWN

People say that they wish someone really knew them, really understood them, really knew what they were going through. Some of the most poignant loneliness in life comes from knowing that no one knows you or what you mean when you try to explain this or that. It's worse when other people *think* they know and tell others—but they're all wrong. Is there no escape from this?

The escape lies in that most private of all human acts: prayer. God knows you from all eternity. God loves you from all eternity. God does not make mistakes.

St. Thomas Aquinas describes prayer as "mutual self-revelation." You tell God about you, knowing that God knows and understands even better than you do. God does not have to hear your concerns in order to understand you. God listens to you because it is good for you and because God loves you.

Look at the story of Jesus and the woman at the well (John 4:1–42). After she told him that she had no husband, Jesus told her everything she ever did. (Notice that the text says "everything." It does not say her sins only.) As a result of this mutual self-revelation, the woman was so full of love that she brought the townspeople to Jesus. They came because of her. They stayed because of him.

Prayer is mutual. You speak. God listens. God speaks. Now you listen. One of the simplest ways of listening is to listen to God's word in Scripture. In particular, attend to Scripture used in the liturgy. Really listen to God's self-revelation. This is prayer. And here you will find friendship.

182

PETITION

When you petition God for a favor, you are somewhat hopeful.

Why should you hope in God? The answer is simple. You can hope in God, St. Thomas Aquinas says, because you belong to God. Just as people tend to take care of those who belong to them, so God takes care of you. Just as you take care of others in your human way, so God takes care of creatures in a divine way. Remember this when you ask God for something. Don't expect to understand God's response!

As much as you hope God will grant what you ask, as much as you don't see any reason God shouldn't do what you ask, as much as you want what you are asking for, try to remind yourself:

~ I know I want this.
~ I know God knows more and better than I.
~ I trust God to give me what is good for me in the eyes of God. I will not insist on what is good for me in my human eyes.
~ I am ever learning that God is God.

If you are up to doing this, do it with a glad heart.

If you are not up to it, spend some time with God about your not being up to it, and ask for what you need. Spend a little time being attentive to GOD.

The more you get used to "sinking" into God, or "free-falling" into God's waiting arms, the more intimate you will be with your God. Then, more and more, you will understand how God's love for you is expressed in this life. You might want to read Luke 11:9–13.

Stay with the Holy Spirit, whose indwelling is your gift.

183

RAGE, GRIEF, ANGUISH—AND THEIR ASSORTED RELATIVES

No matter what the emotion is, it is a strong one. No matter what causes you to suffer, it overcomes you.

You react as you do to severe stress. People close to you react as they do when you are "that way."

Even if you think about praying, have you stopped trying to say how this circumstance really affects you, because words cannot describe what it does to you—right to the core of your being? Or have you been misunderstood so much that you do not want to make yourself vulnerable to another rejection? Or has the power of the emotion left you either too drained to think of anything or too energized to stand still?

However you are, it is a good time to pray. Certainly God knows about your situation. Just as certainly it is good for you to bring yourself for whatever it is that will help and heal you from this suffering.

As consciously as you can, be in your God's presence. (If you don't feel it, do it in faith.) Greet God, and show God your heart, your spirit, *you*. Come without words, without thoughts, without anything but you and how you are now.

Stay like this for as long as you want.

Come back as often as you need to.

Always, always let yourself believe: You *are loved* by your God.

In the end, all will be well. (When you are experienced in God's ways, the pain might not be less, but the assurance is strong. All will be well. How the "well" happens might be a big surprise!)

184

THE FATHER

Jesus is the Word of God, the self-revelation of God. In every one of the Gospels Jesus prays to his Father. In every one of the Gospels Jesus talks about his Father. *Who* is Jesus' Father? *What* is Jesus' Father like? *Why* does Jesus instruct us to pray, "Our Father . . ."? Study what Jesus says:

~ "So it is not the will of your Father in heaven that one of these little ones should be lost" (Matthew 18:14).
~ "Whenever you stand praying, forgive, if you have anything against anyone; so that your Father in heaven may also forgive you your trespasses" (Mark 11:25).
~ "Be merciful, just as your Father is merciful" (Luke 6:36).
~ "But Jesus answered them, 'My Father is still working, and I also am working'" (John 5:17).
~ "Everything that the Father gives me will come to me, and anyone who comes to me I will never drive away" (John 6:37).

God so loved all people that God sent Jesus to tell who God is and what God is like. When you think about it, it is astounding! A basic action of gratitude might be to study what God tells you through Jesus. Then pray as God's Spirit moves you.

Choose a passage concerning what Jesus says about his Father, your God. Empty your mind of everything except the meaning of the passage, its implications. Lose yourself in this revelation of God.

Jesus refers to his Father 274 more times in the Gospels. In Matthew's Gospel, Jesus speaks of his Father 99 times in 68 verses (especially in chapter 6); in Mark, 17 times in 16 verses; in Luke, 42 times in 35 verses; in John, 121 times in 99 verses.

185

BEING IN LOVE

What's it like when you are in love? What is the courtship like, the wanting to ask and wanting to be asked—and the delicious fear of the outcome? What is your attitude toward things when you are in love? How is your disposition when you are in love?

What about being in love with your God?

If this were so, how might you be different? When you deeply believe what you say you believe about God's love, how might it affect your daily life? your disposition and attitude?

God already knows you—totally. God already loves you—faithfully. God already welcomes you and invites you to a greater intimacy. The question is, will you make it mutual? And if you do, what happens?

God teaches you inwardly when you are ready to listen. God lets you know "secrets" that, while not making your life easier, surely make it simpler and far more fulfilling. You receive gifts you cannot earn or deserve or obtain by yourself. These are the gifts of the Holy Spirit.

As a pilgrim on the way home to your God, it is good for you to stay in touch daily. (Jesus says to "pray always and not to lose heart" [Luke 18:1].) For this you need no equipment, no money, not even any special talent. Your socioeconomic status is irrelevant. What counts is:

Are you truly in love?

Let your yearning, your longing, be your prayer before your God.

If you lack it, ask God to give it to you. If you have it, ask God for what you need to adore God as GOD.

186

SURRENDER

Surrender is an unpleasant, not-to-be-thought-about word for some people. It might convey an attitude of failure, of degradation, of inferiority, or of weakness. It also might be a reality that is appropriate and life-giving. Sometimes it is a matter of attitude. You have to judge what is right.

Surrender does not necessarily mean giving up. Nor does surrender necessarily mean giving in. Giving up or giving in might be a good response in some circumstances; in others it could be just plain silly. You have to decide what is the honest thing for you to do.

•

Surrender (at least when it is between you and your God, and sometimes when it involves others) means giving over.

God knows you from all eternity. God loves you from all eternity. God keeps you in existence. God is ultimately and only the one who is in control. Surrendering to God is a very good idea at all times. It helps further the life in abundance that Jesus talked about (see John 10:10).

When you think about it, life is full of surrendering. You surrender to bus drivers and subway motormen and airplane pilots. You surrender to dentists and doctors. You surrender to the cost of things, to HMO restrictions, and to the weather. All of these "surrenders" are intrinsically uncertain.

Surrendering to a loving God, who unequivocally has your good at heart, is a joyously right thing ever and always.

You might, in your God's presence, think about surrender. Then ask God for what your heart wants, not the least of which might be trust and courage.

Really give this time. Thinking deeply about who God is might easily make you fearful. If so, good! God truly is awesome. And God truly loves you and wants to be with you forever. God's "forever" really is forever.

187

BEING WITH ONE YOU LOVE

St. Thomas Aquinas said that you don't know a person until you love that person. Such loving entails contemplation—being attentively present, gazing at the other person intently, thinking lovingly about him or her. Then you not only know about the person; you have experience of the person.

What does it take to contemplate God?

Being with one you love and who loves you. The great saint Teresa of Avila wrote that. Her friend St. John of the Cross said, "Come empty. Do nothing. Only persons who love one another can do that happily."

The joy of it is that God wants *you* to come. God's invitation is always extended to you. Accept it. Open your heart to God. Attend lovingly to each other. After all, this is what all those other ways of praying lead to!

188

FREE FALL

Have you ever watched a child standing on a fence, a diving board, or some high place, being encouraged to fall or jump into waiting arms? If you are watching the child in this situation, you might see the eagerness, the fear, the uncertainty on the child's face. You can see the tense little body moving ahead, withdrawing, uncertain. The child wants to trust, but. . . Sometimes the child can jump into the waiting arms of an encouraging adult. Sometimes the child just cannot do it. Perhaps at one time you were that child.

Have you ever watched (in actual fact, on television, or in a movie) a person free-fall from an airplane? If you have, bring it back to your mind and "see" it again. If you haven't, imagine it. Best of all, if you have done it yourself, relive it.

The following exercise might require a real stretch of your imagination. (Please try it, even if in real life you would not seriously consider jumping from an airplane.)

Consciously remember that you are in the presence of your loving God. Bring yourself, your concerns, your joys, everything about you, into focus.

Then let yourself *free-fall into the arms of your waiting God!* When you have, stay there.

If you can't do it yet, let God know how you feel, and receive the comfort you need.

Then, when you are ready, go!

189

SACRED

Encountering God can be an awe-full, terrifying experience, yet one that is so very right. Encountering God in the interior of your heart and soul can fill you with an intensity of emotion beyond any other experience.

When you have such an encounter, you might be moved to tell someone. This news seems too good to keep to yourself.

On the contrary, it is too good *not* to keep to yourself.

Such rare and extraordinarily privileged moments are of utmost sacredness. Talking about them can weaken them. Besides, not many people will understand what you are talking about—and that will diminish the experience too.

If you have a spiritual director or a steady confessor or an exceptionally spiritual friend, you can confide in that one person. Not more than one, one most carefully chosen.

Guard the deep secrets of your God and you.

How do you know if this experience is really of God, or your own imagination? Always look at the effects of it. How does it affect your relationships with others? Does it make you more compassionate, more generous, more understanding, more wise? "By their fruit you will recognize them" (Matthew 7:20, NIV).